A Book
About Bread

A Book
About Bread

A Baker's Manual

Issa
Niemeijer-Brown

HL ❧ BOOKS

for Leidie, Rudo,
Alex and Ezra

About the author:
Coming from a family with French and Italian
ties, Issa Niemeijer-Brown was raised in a
tradition of home baking that appreciated quality
and simplicity. After graduating cum laude in
Sociology from the University of Amsterdam,
he chose to become a baker. In 2008, following
years acquiring experience at renowned bakeries
in the Netherlands, France, and Italy, Issa and
his brother founded Gebroeders Niemeijer (The
Niemeijer Brothers). Located in the heart of
Amsterdam, the artisanal French bakery quickly
gained international standing and acclaim for its
croissants, pastries, and bread.

At gebroedersniemeijer.nl/blog you will find
instructional videos about turning, shaping,
cutting, and scoring dough.

Copyright © Issa Niemeijer-Brown
Design concept and illustrations:
Rachelle Klaassen
Photography: Inga Powilleit
Copy editor English edition: Kay Dixon
Lay-out and production: Wouter Eertink

isbn 978 94 6471 071 7

This book was first published in Dutch as *Een
boek over brood* in 2020 by Uitgeverij Brandt,
Amsterdam

Table of Contents

This book is different from other bread baking manuals. Rather than simply providing recipes and instructions, it teaches you the process of bread baking and enables you to create your own recipes.

The first sections of the book walk you step by step through the process of making your own bread. In these initial stages, you will familiarize yourself with the processes of making a dough. From there, you will start to practice making bread.

The second section of the book provides the real recipes as we use them in our bakery. These recipes are just starting points, allowing you to try out different techniques and taste how even small modifications in a recipe can produce dramatic differences in flavor.

After a bit of practice, you will find that you don't need the recipes as much anymore. You will be able to devise your own and adjust our recipes or those of others to suit your own tastes. The final chapter guides you through your first experiments in developing your own recipes, with a number of tips on how to get your bread just the way you would like it to be.

Recipes

Making your own choices

Appendix

Prologue

from baking

as a child,

to baking at home,

to baking in a

wood-fired stone oven,

to starting a bakery

Childhood attempts

For me, becoming a baker means fulfilling a passion which originated from childhood attempts at making filled chocolates and all kinds of pastries. I grew up in a family with a very high standard of home cooking. My parents have close friends in Rome, we spent a lot of time in Italy, and we learned to appreciate the hours and hours spent in the kitchen and subsequently at the dinner table.

We also traveled a lot, and I was exposed to breads and pastries all over Europe. We frequently visited my uncle in France, traveling throughout the country and taking long hikes in the mountains. Part of the treat for me was always going to the local bakeries in the mornings, trying out pastries and croissants for breakfast and taking a baguette back home for a picnic in the fields.

At home in the Netherlands, my parents encouraged my culinary interests, and gave me the freedom to use the kitchen anytime I asked for it, though I am sure they had their

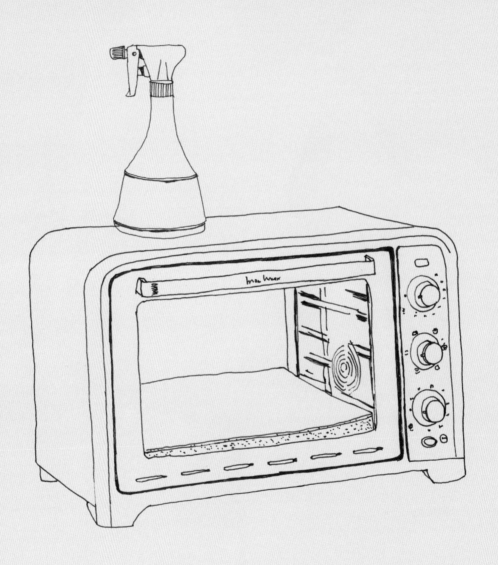

reservations. I loved reading, leafing through my parents' collections of books, which were extensive given their respective careers as a psychologist and an anthropologist. But when baking, I preferred to just look at the pictures in cookbooks. I didn't have the patience to follow actual recipes, I resisted my mother's pressure to think more carefully and plan in advance what I wanted to bake, dismissing her fears of my wasting yet another dough simply because I refused to look up ingredient quantities. But for me this was part of the joy of baking, and anyway I preferred to try to eat half of the cookie and cake batters before they ever made it to the oven.

Becoming a baker was also a matter of coincidence and experimentation. As I grew up, I studied sociology and philosophy, worked in development cooperation, and was involved in reconstruction during and after the war in Bosnia. Over time, I started baking more and more at home, just for fun. I started out with just a Moulinex oven, about the size of a small microwave and with a maximum temperature of 430°F (220°C). As I was advised to do by other home bakers, I put in a baking stone, sprayed the oven interior amply with the plant mister and actually, to my surprise, was able to make really nice baguettes.

Eventually I took it one step further and set out to recreate flavors I remembered from my childhood: the Rosette we had in Rome, French countryside baguettes, sourdough from the Belgian Ardennes.

Though I started reading the recipes as well as looking at the photos, I was not having much success with any of the recipes I found. So, I took a different approach. I tried to understand the precise process of how doughs work, going as far as reading French, American, Swiss, and Italian professional and technical literature on the baking of bread – again, just for the fun of it.

Part-time jobs
As soon as my bread started to become a bit better than average, I was asked to bake for a small deli. I upgraded my oven to a second-hand normal-sized home oven, but one of good quality. Its temperature could reach 570°F (300°C). More

importantly, I could turn the vent on or off and use either heat from below or above. Since it was stronger and sturdier than the previous oven, it contained the heat much better. These qualities helped me to pretend it was an old-fashioned stone oven. While still relatively small-scale, I was able to produce something like thirty baguettes made with a very mild sourdough at home, to be delivered each Saturday at the end of the morning.

Baking at that time looked like this. It would take ten minutes of work to make two doughs at home just before dinner on Friday, benefitting from autolyse, a method intended to reduce kneading times which I had come across through reading the works of the French professor of bakery Raymond Calvel. I used the biggest bowls I had. Then after dinner, I would "fold" both doughs, again drawing on my improved familiarity with French baking techniques (folding is a technique of strengthening and aligning the gluten in a dough). Just before going to bed, I weighed and shaped the loaves, which took about half an hour. I then put them to rest on an improvised *couche*, a sort of blanket made using small baking trays covered with dishtowels. I wrapped the whole thing in large plastic bags and put it in the fridge. The next morning, Saturday, I would wake up at 6:30 a.m. to turn on the oven and preheat the baking stones, go back to bed again, get up again at 7:30 a.m. and put the first batch of bread in the oven. Using two baking stones at the same time, on two layers in the oven, I could bake six small baguettes in one go. At 7:50 a.m., after taking out the first batch of baguettes, I would turn the oven up to maximum heat, and then start baking again at 8:15. At 9:00, a third batch, at 9:45 a.m. a fourth, at 10:30 a.m. a fifth, and then at 11:00 a.m., get on my bike with the bread and race to the deli. All rather laborious, to say the least. In between though, I had plenty of time for a shower, breakfast, and the like – my Saturday morning would in fact be quite relaxed.

At one point I offered my services for a part time job at Hartog, the best Dutch bakery in Amsterdam. After initially being sent away with a "we probably don't need anyone", they called the same evening asking me to come back the next day for an interview. The interview never took place: I was immediately put to work and told I could stay, taking up a curious but not uncommon mixture of tasks for a novice including dishwashing, placing almonds on cookies, and brushing them with egg-wash. I hardly even touched the bread dough, and was never able to make a dough myself or bake a loaf.

Meanwhile I started to bake my own bread and pastries on the weekends for a small Swiss neighborhood restaurant. Here I had the advantage of a larger restaurant oven, so I could bake all the bread needed in two rounds as well as make some cakes and pastries in between. I used a similar routine as I did when baking in my home oven. I made a dough at home before dinner and folded it after dinner. Only now, after giving it some time to rest, I would take the dough on my bike to the restaurant kitchen. I would do the shaping there and leave it in the fridge overnight. I made a number of tiles to fit inside the restaurant oven, to simulate the effects of a stone oven for those few hours in the morning that I was using it.

Acquiring practice

Even after all that time, I found that I could approach, but still not quite reach, the flavors I had in my memory. I was working at a bakery, I had read almost all the baking literature I could lay my hands on. But I was confounded by the huge gaps I encountered between the theoretical knowledge about grain kernels and chemical processes of gluten formation, and the actual daily practice of bread baking based on the information you have at hand at home, or even as a professional baker in a bakery. Flour bags don't often come with an exact technical analysis of flour qualities. So, there I was, back again to childhood days, of experimenting, of just going for it no matter what...

I traveled and visited bakeries in the United States, France, Portugal, Spain, Italy, and Switzerland, talking with the bakers and sometimes also staying to help out for a day or a night – the best way to enjoy being a baker. Apart from learning a lot, this is a wonderful way to get to know people and to feel at home in places you have never been before. Baking alongside someone forges an immediate bond and gives you an insight into their character – somehow everything you do, your mood of the day, is reflected in the bread coming out of the oven.

During my travels I also learned to bake in a wood-fired stone oven. My family had acquired a small farmhouse in southern Portugal, and there we could bake about twelve big loaves in one go. From our neighbors I learned how to make the traditional bread from the Algarve. Manuela showed me how to make the dough while her husband Chico taught me how to build the fire and when to bake. His technique was to light a very hot, big fire, for an hour or so, using mostly thin wood which would burn quickly and give off a lot of heat. Then he would clean out the oven, first with a kind of self-made wooden broom (without the bristles), and then with a damp cloth on a stick. After letting the oven settle for half an hour to an hour, to let the temperature even out and drop again to about 480°F (250°C) (my guess, no thermometer was involved), he would then start baking.

The bread Manuela and Chico baked would be meant to last for up to 10 days, getting drier and drier, but remaining of good quality. It was made of a very basic dough: local flour (type 65), salt, water, and yeast. The crust remained a bit pale as they did not use any steam when baking. It would burst open naturally, a result of the way the loaf was shaped rather than the *grigne* characteristic of French bread. The inside structure remained quite dense. All in all, it was a very nice countryside bread that can be found almost anywhere in Southern Europe, at farms which still have (and use) their stone ovens.

Drawing on my family's Italian upbringing, I didn't waste the "resting time" of the oven before baking the bread. After the oven was heated up, I would leave some of the logs inside the oven, moving them to the side to keep a small fire going. The intense heat made it possible to make incredible pizzas. Then when the oven started to cool down, I would bake the bread.

I didn't succeed in making Parisian baguettes. I tried but could not manage to produce enough steam in the big oven. But by throwing in a little water at the beginning of baking, I found I could get a nice crust and a *grigne* on bigger breads, such as *batards* or *boules*, and a commendable open structure on the inside. The bread was appreciated by our neighbors as well.

Eventually I joined another Dutch baker with a passion for
French bread: Menno 't Hoen's Du Pain bakery in Rotterdam.
Having trained in France, he could teach me the skills required
to shape hundreds of loaves by hand in just a few hours. In him,
I also found a partner in my search to understand what happens
in a dough, and in my search for pure flavors. Together we
experimented in improving recipes.

Eventually, I thought it was time to move to Paris and work
there for a while. I chose Gosselin bakery, which had won
a prize for the best baguette in Paris and had been given
additional fame by Peter Reinhart, who wrote about his visit
to Paris in the introduction to his book *The Bread Baker's
Apprentice*. I have to admit that I forgot to mention in my
application that I lacked official bakery schooling. The
omission gave me the opportunity to step right in, regardless of

hierarchy, and work in the bread bakery as well as make pastries and croissants. In a short time, I was able to gain hands-on experience in all the areas that interested me.

Becoming professional

When I returned home from Paris, the bread I baked using my own recipes became better and better, finally recreating the flavors of my childhood memories. I now understood why the bread in almost all bakeries seldom resembled the breads I remembered from the past. And I understood how to create the flavors I was searching for. My brother, who was working as a chef, proposed that we start our own bakery and café.

It was quite a leap of faith. We borrowed €250,000, rented a historic building in the center of Amsterdam, put in floors, tiled the walls, painted, bought second-hand chairs, and made tables, designed a counter. On top of that we purchased a whole range of equipment, from a French stone oven to work surfaces, proofing cabinets, a dough mixer, fridges, and more.

Sourcing flour proved a difficult task. We visited *Europain*, the yearly international bakery convention held in Paris. However, all of the stands were aimed at formula baking, offering machines and bakery ingredients which were meant to facilitate the process, rather than improve quality – and accordingly, the flour mills mostly offered pre-made mixes, or flour loaded with ameliorants. Not satisfied, I subsequently visited several smaller mills in France which offered stone-ground and organic flours without additives. I asked for samples from the three mills that seemed the most promising, to try out.

The bread recipes I had developed and which we wanted to use in our bakery had so far only been tried out at home – working with the home oven, using the fridge instead of proofing cabinets, and with flour from the supermarket and organic shops. I had never made any of them on a large scale.

Finally, less than a week before our bakery opened, all the equipment was installed, and I could start testing. After two tries we chose the flour that seemed to work best, drove to France with a rental van and brought back 900 kilos, the

maximum the van could carry. With the bakery opening in a matter of days there was one more chance to make a trial run, now using the new flour. The breads were still far from how I wanted them to be. I made adjustments to the recipes and started again.

When our bakery opened the next day, it worked! The three trial runs had provided just enough information about how to use the flour, the proofing cabinets, the oven... The breads were beautiful. The croissants turned out just as I had imagined and so did the pastries. For the first time, we could fill up the shop with baked goods, offering breakfast and lunch. Customers very quickly became regulars and we immediately received positive reviews in journals and magazines. On Saturdays people started queueing up. Everything worked, was good enough, and slowly I could make further improvements and develop new recipes.

That first year, my days started at 6:30 a.m., working mostly by myself in the bakery while my brother ran the shop and

café. I did get much-appreciated help from friends, who in turn became expert bakers over time. In the morning I started baking immediately, using the small windows of time when the bread and croissants were in the oven to prepare pastries. Around 9:00 a.m. I started the first dough, around 10:30 a.m. two more and around 11:30 a.m. the last one. At 1:00 pm I began weighing and shaping the loaves, which could take until 4:00 p.m. The timing was designed for a slow, cold rise aimed at having the bread at the right stage of development the next morning. That process differs markedly from the usual practice in other bakeries, where the final phase of proofing is done at a higher temperature. In between all of this I continued baking fresh baguettes and pastries for the shop and making doughs for croissants and brioche. In the late afternoon and evening, I refreshed the sourdough, folded the croissant dough, prepared pastries, made macarons, and in the end, shaped the croissants and brioche, all to be baked the next morning. Around 11:00 p.m. I would be ready for the following day.

And now

Now, my days look different. Instead of working alone, two
or three bakers work together, or even four on busy days.
Sometimes the servers in the café help with tasks in the bakery
as well, making the crammed workspace as crowded and busy
as a beehive. Our oven is relatively small for the quantities of
bread we bake, and since customers start arriving in the early
morning, we need to begin early. The first baker starts around
5:00 or 6:00 a.m. The others arrive later to help weigh and
shape the loaves – up to six or seven hundred a day. We have
learned how to fit in all the pastry preparations between rounds
of bread baking, by using every minute to the maximum. Now,
we bake the last round of breads and pastries around 3:00 p.m.
and finish the day around that time as well. The work is hectic,
intense, and lively. We alternate continually between baking,
washing the dishes, making bread doughs, preparing pastries,
and, at busy moments, even helping in the shop or serving
guests in the café – sometimes all at the same time.

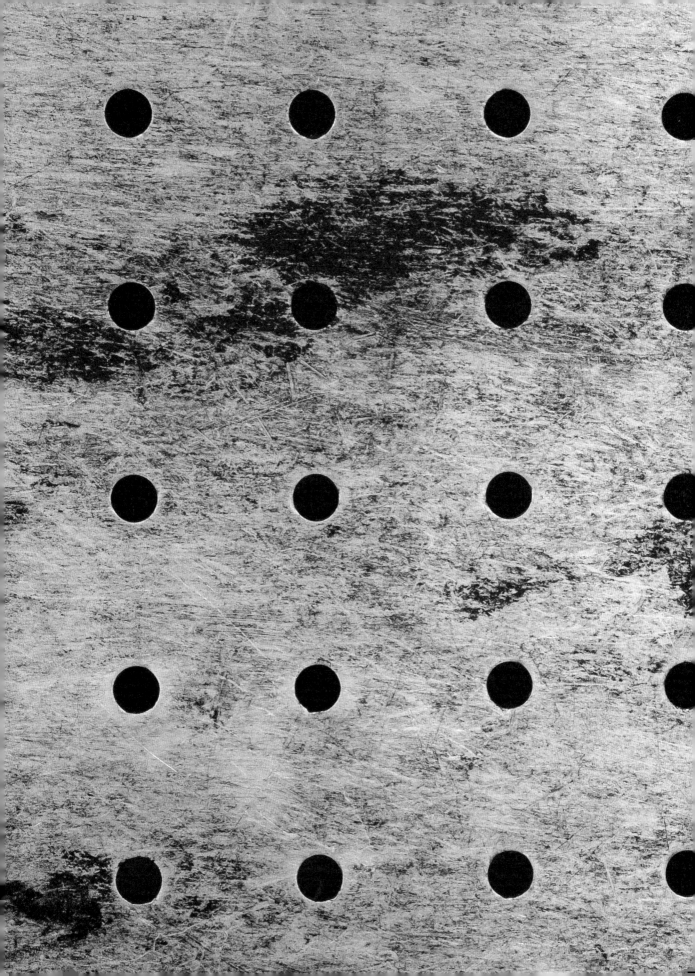

Introduction

French baking – reinventing tradition

What is it about French bread? It has to do with romance, probably. A baguette in Paris tastes better than a baguette anywhere else, simply because it is in Paris, wrapped in paper, fresh from the baker's oven, picked up on the way back from work, and carried home for dinner. But part of that romance derives from the *finesse* with which some of the French enjoy life – the pure flavors of the dinner to which the baguette is essential, and the time taken to savor the meal. The crunch the baguette provides when broken – not sliced – and shared at the table. The balance it lends to the cheeses taken out for dessert. The baguette is made to match all of this – simple and pure.

An appreciation for purity and simplicity is not unique to France. In Southern Italy, for instance, traditional cooking is based on pure flavors as well. Breads sometimes incorporate Italian ingredients such as *grano duro* (strong pasta flour), potatoes, or olive oil, but very often just stick to the basics of flour, water, and salt. Rural breads in Germany are of high quality as well, combining simplicity and flavor, though they are much more robust and solid, rather than light and delicate like the Parisian baguette.

Since the development of modern bakery techniques, and especially the commercialization of baking, these kinds of traditional breads are increasingly difficult to find anywhere in Europe, even in Paris or rural France and Italy. Flour mills produce pre-made flour mixes, bakeries are speeding up their processes and traditional knowledge is being replaced by that of a growing industry, focused on formulas that can be sold and easily applied in the form of bakery chains, such as Le Pain Quotidien, Paul, and others.

One of the most important books on bread making in France, *Le Goût du Pain* (*The Flavor of Bread*), was written in 1990 to counterbalance these trends in their initial phases. The book tried to embrace modernization, without losing the characteristics of French bread, most notably its flavor. A foundation to promote this work still exists and its value remains undisputed. And yet it is abroad, in highly industrialized countries with a very poor historical tradition of bread making, such as the United States or the United Kingdom,

that the search for traditional, artisan bread made by hand and baked in stone ovens has flourished. In the French countryside, most bakeries do not search for artisanship so much as strive for modernization, and to improve production facilities and working conditions. In urban centers like Paris, where there is the largest potential clientele of gourmands, any baker with artisanal flair gains popularity so quickly that quality soon gives way to quantity and mass production – reducing their products to yet another concept to be exported.

An apparent exaltation of the traditional is easy to see at bakeries throughout Europe. Yet – for the most part – there is nothing "real" or "traditional" about this trend. These bakeries share a mix of appropriate lighting (with a touch of yellow), calculated pricing (slightly on the expensive side), and a décor involving wood veneer benches and factory-produced wicker baskets. Every now and then a label claiming "home-made" or "artisanal" status is prominently displayed. But of course, these are not always protected labels. What about "home made on a large scale in our factory by people operating machines"? Or "organic" claims which merely signify the origin of ingredients without providing any information on the production process or the product quality? Even a supermarket gets away with just the same techniques. In other words, "tradition" in the artisan bakery trend is produced using contemporary production techniques, supported by contemporary marketing techniques. It is becoming ever harder to find something truly traditional.

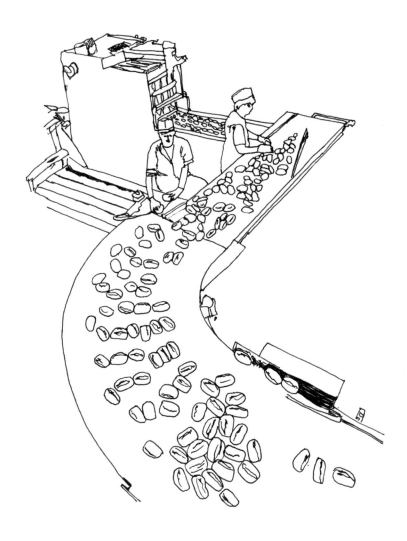

This raises a further question, what precisely is "traditional"? Was bread in the past constantly of the same quality? Or did bakers in the past always sprinkle some extra flour on top of their bread to make it look artisanal? Did customers want to buy the best bread, not caring about the price? The answer to all of these questions is a straightforward "no". But it is true that, historically, bread was produced under different circumstances, which led to different results and different flavors than we currently find. Baking machines of the first half of the twentieth century did not allow for the same intensive kneading that is common today. Labor was relatively inexpensive. Flour wasn't manipulated with the same technological skill. Ovens were floor ovens rather than rotary ovens. Bakeries were organized differently: as individual, independent enterprises, based on the artisanal skills (or the lack thereof) of the baker and his assistants. Customers did not expect the same regularity, continuity, or consistency of the bread that supermarkets have accustomed them to.

My choices as a baker

In this book, as in our bakery, I try to select what I think is best from "tradition" – combining historical knowledge with modern-day appreciation of artisanship, of quality, of preference for the organic, using traditional techniques and advocating the weighing and shaping of bread by hand, even in a professional setting. Not because of its nostalgic value, but simply because it does lead to the highest possible quality. Flavor *is* lost when modern production methods or technically manipulated ingredients are used. From the spate of recent "advances" only one is valuable to me: the use of fridges or proofing cabinets with perfect control of humidity at lower temperatures. Proofing cabinets make it possible to lengthen the development time of a dough and to influence the chemical processes in that development in a manner and with an ease that was not previously possible.

In terms of ideal structure and ideal flavor, my preference lies with French tradition, but also borrows from Italian and sometimes from German, Portuguese, Swiss, Belgian, and North American baking. It involves bread which has an open, airy, irregular structure while being firm at the same time, and a rich crust. I am most interested in producing quality through simplicity, baking bread which may be an accompaniment and complement to meals, or eaten on its own, just as it is.

There's one further point to touch on. Coming from the Netherlands and having studied at university, I write this book from a different perspective than a French baker, or someone born into a family of bakers. I am not trying to move away or "climb the social ladder" from a quite hard, demanding physical job, or, in a similar vein, trying to reduce the work to a minimum. I actually enjoy the physical and manual work. I felt at home in the underground caves of the Gosselin bakery, and it is the artisanal qualities of bread that I appreciate most. Baking gives me a sense of freedom, rather than constraint.

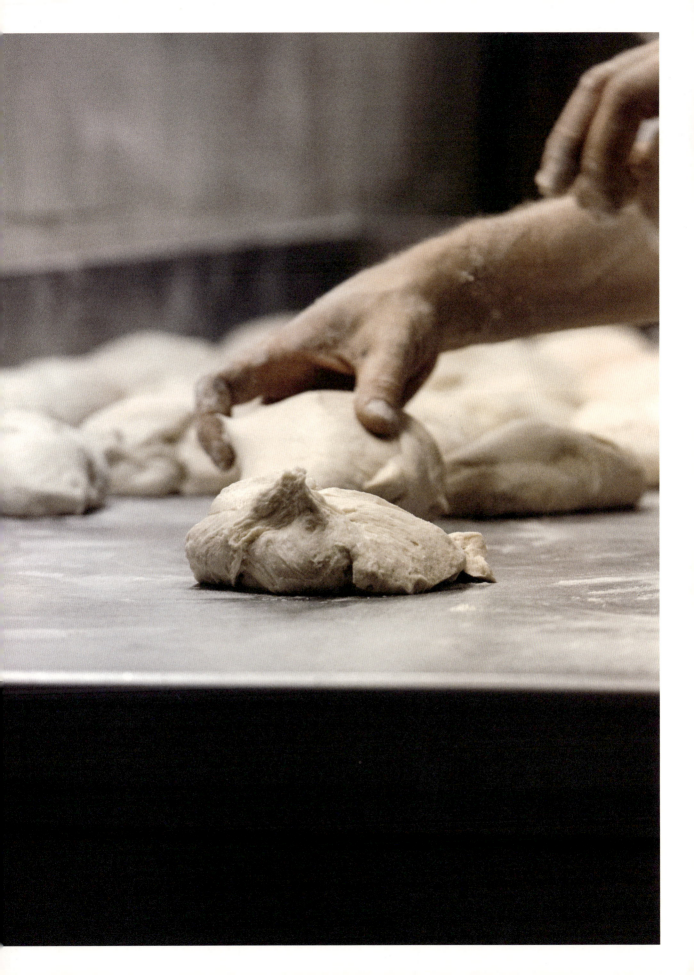

Defining bread

Ingredients

To make bread you need flour, water, salt, and a leavening agent such as yeast or sourdough. These four ingredients are all you need to produce an infinite variety of different breads.

Wheat is the most common flour used for bread baking. This is not an arbitrary choice. The proteins present in wheat have the ability to form gluten, very thin networks of protein which are able to contain gases, while other flours often don't have this potential. Hence, even when grains such as rye, barley, maize, or buckwheat are used in bread, they are usually mixed with wheat.

To bind the flour, and also to set in motion a number of chemical and physical reactions elementary to the development of bread, the addition of some kind of liquid is essential. Water, because of its purity, is the most commonly used. It doesn't contain any fats, sugars, acids, or other agents which would influence the nature of the bread. And historically speaking, water was and is one of the most easily and widely available resources in Europe. But other liquids can be used. For instance, milk would be another possible choice, producing a bread which is much softer and whose structure is less open, more cake-like. Wine, beer, cider, yogurt, and sour milk can also be used.

Salt mainly serves as a flavoring agent, but as discussed later, it also has an impact on a number of processes taking place in the bread. It is not always used, and some Italian breads are made without. However, though not essential, salt greatly increases the quality of most types of bread.

The leavening agent used in bread is usually yeast (commercial or natural), as is the case when working with sourdough. It makes it possible for the dough to become airy, soft, and more voluminous. However, there are also a large number of very good flatbreads, from, for instance, the Indian, Mexican, African, Arab, or Jewish traditions which do not use any leavening agent. Furthermore, it is possible to make bread with baking powder as a leavening agent as well. Yeast, however, is what brings bread to life – it is literally organisms at work – and to me distinguishes bread from cakes or pastries. It doesn't just make the dough expand, it produces a specific flavor while it is working inside the dough, a flavor anyone used to European or North American bread (or, for instance, North African or Indian yeasted flatbreads) would immediately recognize.

Wheat

Photo: Thomas has just folded the baguette dough

Taking, for present purposes, yeast as the definitive ingredient of bread, it follows that the definitive dimension of bread baking processes is the time allowed for yeast to enable the dough to develop, to do its work. Yeast doesn't work instantly, it needs time to make a dough expand.

Baking is a second crucial component in what makes a bread. Without heat, dough stays raw and is only edible in very small amounts. Furthermore, without heat, the dough development would continue until it breaks itself down. Baking also largely determines bread's characteristic flavor and smell, because of chemical reactions that only take place with intense heat.

It is important to be aware that the kind of "European" bread that is explored in this book was exported to former colonial empires. In many countries it partly replaced local products or varieties. To some extent, it has been "globalized" – and though now it seems universal to many of us, this is actually not the case.

Yeast and sourdough

One of the most basic distinctions between different kinds of bread is between a bread made with yeast and one with sourdough. What exactly is the difference between these two types of bread?

Yeast is a specific kind of organism, which digests sugars in the dough and produces carbon dioxide gases in doing so. Carbon dioxide causes the dough to rise as these gases become embedded in the dough's gluten network (the layers of proteins present in the flour, which start to develop the moment it mixes with water).

There are different species of yeast. The commercially available variety is known as "baker's yeast", and can be purchased in dried form or as blocks of "fresh" yeast. It works relatively fast, enabling the speedy development of a dough. As a consequence, breads made with yeast tend to develop quickly and have corresponding characteristics: lightness, a large volume, but also a very soft crumb and thin crust, and a mild, if not bland, flavor. This problem can be mitigated by using very small amounts of yeast, thus enabling a longer development process for the dough. In that way flavor can become much more pronounced, pure, and delicate, and the crust stronger.

Sourdough also contains yeast, but of a different species. It is a natural yeast which is present in grains, or even in the air, and is cultivated by providing a suitable environment for its growth. The concentration of sourdough yeast is not as high as baker's yeast, and the development speed of a bread made with sourdough is relatively slow, when compared to that of a bread made with commercial yeast (although it also depends on the quantities used, of course). One characteristic of the yeast in a sourdough is that it tolerates a higher level of acidity. If you were to add commercial yeast to a sourdough to speed up the process, as is common practice in many bakeries, it would work very well for a few hours, but, with time, it would eventually be overpowered by the natural yeasts in the sourdough which can better withstand the increasing acidity in the dough.

In addition to natural yeast, sourdough also contains a rich culture of bacteria, which are in part responsible for the creation of acidity in the dough, as well as for the production of volatile organic fatty acids which lend the bread a complex palette of flavors. The acidity has the effect of preserving the bread, causing the crumb to stay fresh much longer. It also works on the grains to break them down, predigest them and make them more easily digestible for us.

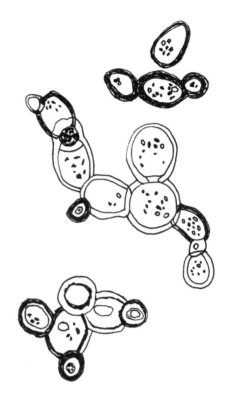

Baker's yeast molecules

It is often assumed that eating sourdough bread is healthier than bread made with commercial yeast. This depends in large part on the production methods. Bread made with a small quantity of yeast which has developed slowly can sometimes be more easily digestible than sourdough bread that has been produced without taking the proper time. Likewise, yeast bread made of organic stoneground flour which has been subjected to minimal kneading can contain more nutrients than an intensively kneaded sourdough bread made with industrially ground flour.

Interestingly, the French word for sourdough, *levain,* just means "raising agent" and does not refer to acidity. Depending on how you use sourdough, it is possible to control the acidic flavor, while keeping its quality as both a leavening and a preserving agent. Because bread made with sourdough develops more slowly, flavor will generally be richer and fuller, and the crust stronger. Sourdough bread might not be as light as bread made with commercial yeast, but it can actually still have a very open and airy structure. Sourdough bread might not be as light as bread made with commercial yeast, but it can actually still have a very open and airy structure. That is because these qualities depend not so much on the type of yeast used, as on the balance of ingredients, and the choices you make when kneading, shaping, and letting the dough develop, and when baking the bread.

When a sourdough bread and a yeast bread are allowed to develop in full, the yeasted bread will taste of fresh grain, with a hint of nuts. The flavor comes from "roasted" proteins in the flour, and the delicate sweetness from the sugars developed in the dough and caramelized in the crust while baking – very pure flavors. The sourdough bread will have a more pronounced or mildly acidic flavor, but will always be very rich, strong, and full-bodied. In both cases, chemical reactions taking place in the crust while baking at a high temperature produce allegiances between proteins and sugars which are characteristic for the flavor of any good bread, and which provide the recognizable smell of bread baking in the oven.

Wholemeal, multigrain, and white bread

Photo: white, and walnut and fig petits pains

Many people in North America and in northern or western European countries associate dark or multigrain bread with wholemeal bread, and wholemeal bread with healthy, nutritive bread. Many people also like their bread to be light and airy. Bakers know this, manufacturers of flour mixes know this, marketing engineers of supermarkets know this, and all are happy to advocate the possibility of light, airy, wholemeal bread – even though it is not possible to have all these qualities at the same time.

In actual fact, wholemeal bread is always heavier than white bread. The color of a bread loaf is not indicative of the kind of flour it has been made of, nor does it guarantee a higher nutritive value. The dark color is often achieved by adding burned malt to a white bread dough, thus giving it the light texture of white bread, but the "healthy" color of whole grain. A handful of grains added to the dough make it "multigrain".

The assumption that real wholemeal bread is healthier than white bread is questionable too. Wholemeal bread always contains more fiber, and for those of us who have a diet generally lacking in fiber, it would probably be advisable to eat wholemeal bread. In countries like France, Portugal, Spain and Italy, however,

and also in Mediterranean Northern Africa, people generally eat white bread, taking their fiber from other sources, such as vegetables or fruits. In terms of vitamins and minerals, what is more important is the way the flour is milled and the way the bread is produced. Stone-ground flour contains more oil than flour ground in cylinder mills – the most common method for industrially produced flours. And fewer minerals and vitamins are lost during grinding in a stone mill.

The most important factor in determining the health value of the bread is, however, the intensity of kneading while making the dough. In many bakeries, in order to produce lightness and a regular crumb in less time, dough made of white flour is kneaded intensively, leading to the oxidation and loss of many of its vitamins. The dough is literally bleached by the intensive kneading. The result is a perfectly white supermarket bread, but a dark looking multigrain bread can be made just as easily with the same dough. When subjecting wholemeal flour to the same kind of intensive kneading, fiber is retained, but vitamins (and flavor) will be lost just the same.

Healthy or unhealthy?

In recent times some people have contended that it is better not to eat bread at all. To some, bread represents gluten and fast-acting carbohydrates and is assumed to be hard to digest. This is a very reasonable line of thought, when looking at the bread that is commonly available in supermarkets, and even in many "old-fashioned" bakeries, where bread is produced in a way that is very similar to that of industrially made bread. Even fashionable contemporary bakeries often work in the same way, albeit with a more artisanal presentation. The resulting bread has very little nutritive value – apart from the carbohydrates – and because of the fast development process the grains have hardly been "pre-digested", making it heavy on the digestive system. Moreover, all kinds of additives are used that not everyone can digest easily, such as lactose or extra gluten, and grain strands are manipulated to contain more protein, leading to a higher gluten content.

At the same time, bread that has been made with stone-ground flour and allowed to develop slowly – giving the acids in the dough time to break down the gluten and predigest the flour – and with minimal kneading, can be both more easily digestible and a very rich source of nutrients, full of minerals, vitamins and protein. The rising popularity of spelt flour (for bread, but also in a wide range of products such as cake, muesli, cookies, and croissants) should be interpreted in this context. The flour supplier, and in turn the baker or the supermarket, leads customers to believe that products made with spelt flour are healthier than those made with wheat flour. Often, spelt is presented as even suitable for people who are gluten intolerant. It is said to be more natural and authentic – thus simultaneously making it possible to raise the price of the product.

But this rationale neglects the fact that it is mainly the production process that determines the relative digestibility of a loaf of bread. The chemical difference between spelt and regular wheat flour is minimal, and "pure" spelt (that has not been cross-bred with regular wheat) is a rarity. Unless someone suffers from a very specific allergy, there is little reason to favor spelt. Both kinds of wheat contain proteins that form gluten, and the gluten content is more dependent on the intensity of kneading, the time allowed for the dough to rise, the acidity of the dough, and on whether extra-strong varieties of wheat are chosen, or whether gluten is added by the baker or the flour mill.

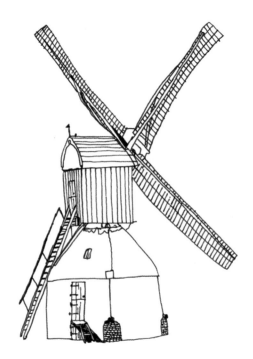

My choices

As a baker I choose to advocate production methods which maintain and enhance the nutritive value, but also the *flavor* of any kind of flour. Rather than making multigrain bread, I like to develop the flavor of the flour itself to its maximum. I bake wholemeal bread precisely for its distinctive and dominant flavor, characterized by the strong presence of fiber. I also bake white bread and "grey" bread made of flour which is in between wholemeal and white flour. The lower proportion of fiber present in white and grey bread provides scope for other, more subtle flavors to rise to prominence. The choice of flour also depends on the food you would like to combine with the bread. For cheese fondue I would definitely choose a baguette, while for a vegetable sandwich grey sourdough bread is perfect. Being influenced by French and Mediterranean cuisine, I generally favor different varieties of white bread over wholemeal, preferring their ability to counterbalance and accompany many flavors without dominating.

Making your
own bread –
what you need
to know

The easiest bread to make comes down to the mixing of water, flour, salt, and a raising agent such as a homemade sourdough or commercial yeast, leaving it to rest for some time, and then putting it in a well preheated oven. By focusing on the way these steps are carried out, and possibly including shaping as a fourth step, it is possible to make a wide range of high-quality breads, with very diverse characteristics.

I will explain these steps one by one: mixing, letting the dough rest and rise, shaping (optional), and baking. The aim here is to understand what happens as you work on a dough, so that later you will be able to see what happens when you try out some of the recipes from our bakery – and maybe you will even be able to predict how the bread tastes, looks, feels and smells, just by observing the ingredients and procedures used.

First, I will explain some things about the basic ingredients to be used.

Choosing flour, salt, and yeast; using water

Before you start to bake bread, you need to buy flour, salt, and yeast. Here we elaborate a bit on possible choices when selecting ingredients, and also the consequences of using various types of flours, or different amounts of water.

Flour

We'll start off with flour, the first ingredient you need when making a dough. At this point it's good to know that every type of flour has different characteristics, needs different treatment, and leads to a different final result. In the appendix we explain a bit more about the technical specifications you are looking for if you want to take it that far. Here, I will just give you a general idea of the range of choices available.

"All-purpose flour" doesn't really exist. If a package is labeled this way, it is unlikely to be really appropriate for any use. Still, if you have no option, take it anyway: before immersing myself fully in baking I used this kind of flour as well. A pastry will not have the same crumbliness as a pastry flour would have given it, a bread will not have the same open structure or quality of

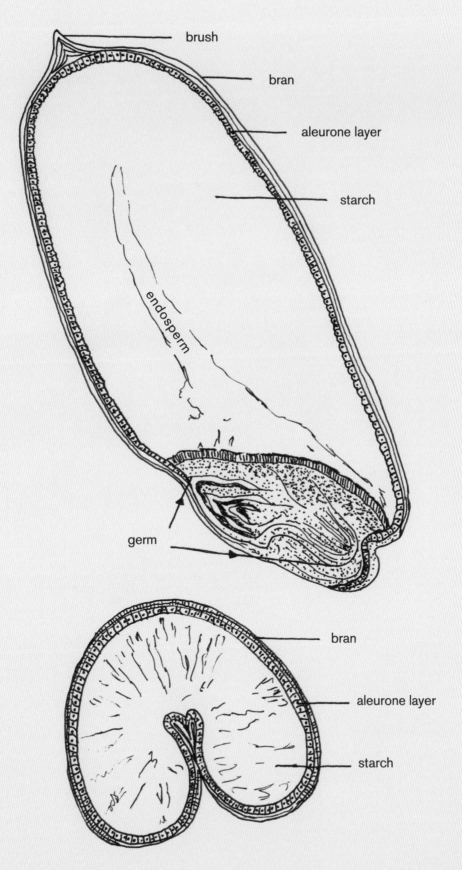

brush

bran

aleurone layer

starch

endosperm

germ

bran

aleurone layer

starch

Cross section of a wheat kernel

crust as a proper bread flour would have provided. It might be denser, or flatten out during its development or while baking. But, given proper care, the result will still be better than bread from the supermarket, and certainly worth the trouble of baking.

Back to the present purpose: bread. If possible, choose flour labeled "bread flour" or "flour for white bread", "wholemeal bread" et cetera. This refers mostly to the amount and the qualities of the proteins present in the flour. These proteins are needed to form the gluten network that keeps the bread together and traps gases that are formed during the development and baking of the dough.

If you are buying flour from the supermarket, try to avoid pre-made mixes, and make sure there are not too many additives. Ascorbic acid would be okay (it's basically vitamin C), and it actually has some positive effects in preserving the original flavor of the flour as it develops into bread. Amylase is nothing to be fearful of either: it's an enzyme normally present in flour and essential to its transformation into bread, and sometimes it is added to the flour at the mill if there wasn't enough amylase in the flour to begin with. Do avoid any substances intended to whiten or bleach either the flour or the dough, as well as sugars (such as lactose) and fats.

If you go to a flour mill, or to an artisanal bakery that doesn't use prefabricated flour mixes, you can try to be more specific: e.g. ask for bread flour suitable for baguettes (extensible, not too elastic, not too strong), for flour ground at least two weeks ago but preferably about a month ago (the flour will have acquired a bit of natural strength, be less sticky and therefore be easier to use and will provide you with a better result), or, if you will be baking it in a tin or Dutch oven, ask for freshly ground flour (providing you with maximum flavor, but a very difficult to handle dough).

The difference between stoneground flour and roller milled flour is essential to its qualities. Roller milling is the standard; if nothing is specified it is (unfortunately) safe to assume the flour has been ground this way – to the detriment of flavor and nutritional value. The grain kernel is split into different parts and the germ – which contains a lot of oil but also many nutrients – is separated and left out to extend its shelf life. Wholegrain flour is then produced by re-adding fibers at the end of the process. When flour is stoneground, the whole grain kernel is ground, and no parts are taken out.

There's also the well-known difference between wholegrain and white flours, discussed before. Wholemeal flour is flour which hasn't been passed through a sieve after being ground, and thus contains not only the kernel but also all the fiber in the grain. White flour has been passed through a series of consecutive sieves, until all the fiber has been removed. However, in France and in some other countries, it's possible to get a far more precise choice. In France, wholemeal flour is known as T150 (type 150), while white flour is known as T55. The number refers to the quantity of ash that would remain after burning the flour completely: the more fiber, the more ash. Then there is also a T80 (a slightly grayish flour, popularly known as *bise*), T65 (a white flour still containing a bit of fiber, and the entire kernel with all its vitamins and minerals) often used for more traditional baguettes and breads, T45 (a very fine flour, suitable for pastries, *viennoiserie*, or bread depending on the quality of its proteins). In principle, it is possible to acquire any kind of flour in between, simply by sieving it a bit more or less. If not available commercially, it is also possible to sieve wholemeal flour at home to reach the required level of fineness. It is also possible to mix wholemeal flour with white flour, although the effect is not the same, as the amount of fiber will be reduced but the size of the fiber will be that of the original wholemeal flour.

In the appendix (p. 222) you can read more about the technical qualities of flour

Finally, even white flour is not literally white. It has a slightly beige, yellowish color deriving from beta carotene, the intensity of which also depends on the original species of grains used – it only becomes white for two reasons: chemical bleaching of the flour before it is sold to you, or your bleaching the flour during the process of bread making by choosing procedures I would not recommend.

White, grey, and wholemeal flour

Water

Water is one of the most readily available ingredients, yet easy to forget in a book about baking breads. It's nevertheless of crucial importance and deserves a special mention. The type or the quality of water is unimportant, as long as it has no strong flavors, and is pure from a nutritive viewpoint. Plain tap water will usually do.

The *amount* of water used, however, is crucial. It is not just that water makes dough drier or wetter, stronger or softer. Water also affects the speed at which chemical processes take place inside the dough. The availability of water increases the speed at which yeast operates, causing the dough to develop faster. It also speeds up the enzymatic activity in dough, thus contributing to its rich flavor. Water also slows down mixing processes, as it becomes harder for the proteins in the flour to encounter each other and form networks of gluten. It greatly affects the extensibility and elasticity of doughs. Doughs with more water are more easily extensible; however, they lose their shape more easily and tend to flatten.

At this point it should be mentioned that the ideal water quantity is closely linked to the characteristics of the flour with which it is combined. Some flours can absorb much more water than others. Some flours have such high enzymatic activity that using too much water causes the dough to develop too quickly or lose its strength and flatten. Yet at the same time, increasing the amount of water in a recipe even slightly can improve a flour which seems to lack "life" or "activity".

Salt

Basically, any ordinary type of salt will do, as long as the grains are not too big. They should easily dissolve into the dough. In our bakery, we prefer to use unrefined sea salt – a French salt from Guerande which dissolves easily and has a full balanced flavor. Refined salt works perfectly well but often has a sharper flavor and just doesn't contribute much to the bread except its saltiness.

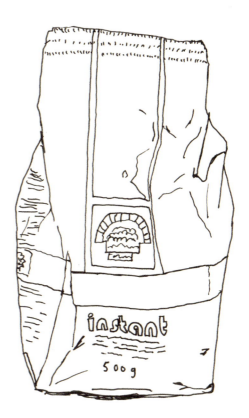

Yeast

This leaves us with yeast. There are three types available: fresh yeast, dried yeast, and instant yeast.

Fresh yeast

has byproducts added to it in order to keep the yeast fresh; its flavor is thus less pure, and you also need more of it. There's nothing wrong in using it, but also no reason to do so.

Dried yeast

is the type which first needs to be dissolved in water. This is the least desirable option. Having to first dissolve the yeast, however simple this sounds, complicates the process. But more importantly, it usually has an unpleasant taste and in my experience is the least reliable. It is just not the right way of treating and keeping yeast.

Instant yeast,

whatever associations the name might conjure up, is actually the purest product. You need the least of it (one third the quantity of fresh yeast), it is both easy to keep and easy to use, and it doesn't bring with it any unwanted flavors. In all of the recipes in this book, it's assumed that you are using this type of yeast. If you are using fresh yeast, simply triple the quantity, and if for any reason you are using dried yeast, double it (and first dissolve the yeast).

Kneading, mixing, and autolyse

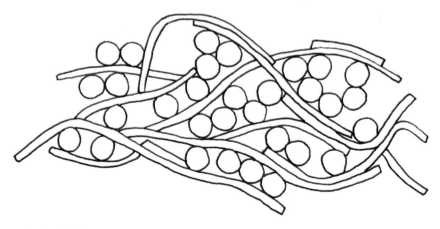

A gluten network starts to develop in the flour as soon as water has been added

What happens during kneading, advantages of autolyse, intensity of mixing

To make the dough, start by adding all the ingredients and mixing them together. The choices made here, in this initial step, greatly affect the final bread. These processes may seem complicated at times. However, the moment you start baking yourself and can feel and see the dough at each step, you will find that what is described matches exactly what is happening in your own hands. It will immediately become much easier to understand.

Usually, a dough is kneaded to develop a strong gluten network, providing sufficient strength to a dough so it can hold its shape and retain the gases produced by yeast. To achieve high quality bread, it may be better to avoid kneading or keep the kneading to a minimum – just enough to mix the ingredients. During kneading, flour oxidizes, losing its color, vitamins and minerals, and, moreover, its flavor. Furthermore, the more dough is kneaded the more the internal texture of the bread will become fine, rather than open. For most of the breads in this book, the ideal texture is that of an open, irregular crumb with smaller and larger alveoli alternating with each other. If you want the texture to be finer, simply increasing the kneading will do the trick.

For almost any kind of bread, I recommend using a method known as autolyse. This method was developed by the French baker and professor Raymond Calvel. It involves allowing the chemical processes which take place in dough to occur by themselves, rather than stimulating them through intensive kneading. The process has the advantage of reducing the amount of time and energy spent kneading the dough, and moreover greatly helps to preserve the qualities of the flour. Minimizing kneading is the first step in reducing oxidation. The autolyse method also helps you to incorporate more water into the dough than would have been possible otherwise. Consequently, the dough is more workable, as the flour has been given the time to absorb the water fully before mixing for the second time.

The amount of kneading and the time given in the resting phase afterwards are strongly correlated. The gluten network requires either time or intense kneading to develop. The more time the dough is given, the less kneading it requires to achieve the same level of development. Thus, the second step to avoid intensive kneading is to provide the dough with a long resting time.

There are more elements to consider: different kneading techniques have a different impact on both the structure of the final bread and on the level of oxidation of the dough. The order in which certain ingredients, most notably yeast, salt, and (if used) fats are added also affects the final structure of the bread. But for now, let's hold back a bit on these considerations and first establish a basic mixing process using the autolyse technique.

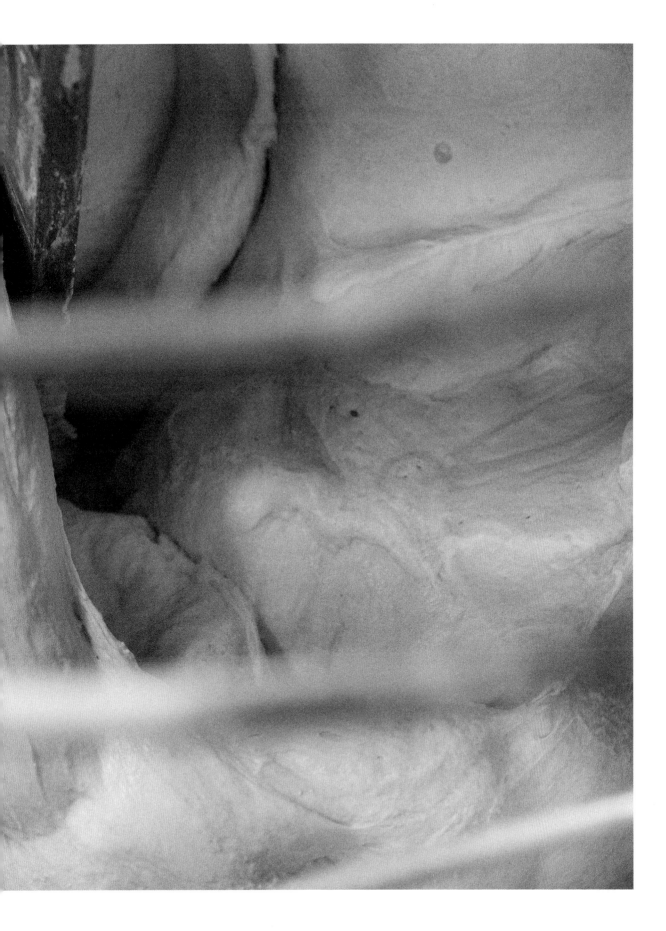

Going for it:
a basic procedure

The simplest way of producing a dough using autolyse rather than intensive kneading is this:

Mix flour and water just until the flour is "hydrated", in other words, all the flour has absorbed some water and there are no dry parts in the dough anymore. This first step is really only about mixing, the dough should not be kneaded yet and should be handled as little as possible. Cover the dough and leave it to stand. Half an hour will generally do the trick and is a good rule of thumb (the ideal resting time will depend on the recipe and the quality of the flour, and any time between 20 minutes and 24 hours is possible for resting the dough). Several processes take place during this half hour. The flour kernels continue absorbing water; the proteins in the flour begin to form gluten networks; and the amylase enzyme in the flour starts to transform starch into sugars – in other words, autolyse is taking place.

When you then start to work on the dough, you will feel that it is less sticky and has more consistency. Now mix in salt, and as soon as the salt is no longer visible on the surface of the dough, yeast. It is important not to mix in the salt and the yeast at the same time, as they should not be in direct contact with each other – the salt will kill the yeast. It is enough to work on the dough until both salt and yeast are well incorporated and mixed in. It is not necessary to work the dough until you have a pre-specified consistency, unless you are in a hurry and can't give it its proper resting time. The latter is the case in most bakeries, and dough is thus kneaded until it is almost ready to bake, at the expense of flavor and quality.

More on the order of adding ingredients (salt and fats)

Now to get back to kneading techniques and the order of adding ingredients.

Salt works as a protective agent, slowing down the oxidation process of vitamins and minerals. If you knead a dough intensively without adding salt, it is "whitewashed". When whitewashing occurs, the beta carotene from which the flour's color derives oxidizes even more easily and the flour loses flavor and nutritive values almost completely. It will however very quickly achieve the required strength for baking, making this a technique commonly used in commercial baking. However, to retain the flour's original qualities, I recommend adding the salt before starting to knead, precisely to avoid "whitewashing" the dough.

Salt also impacts the qualities of the gluten networks as they develop in the dough. Apart from strengthening them, it tends to make them less extensible. This in turn impacts the final bread, which will have less volume and smaller alveoli, and the ease with which the bread can be shaped. In other words, to make a high-quality bread, the perfect moment for adding salt is between the end of the autolyse and the start of kneading. This strikes the balance of avoiding whitewashing the flour while allowing the gluten to become extensible and protecting the dough from oxidation.

Finally, salt also slows down the speed at which the yeast works on the dough. If you were to add yeast before the autolyse, the dough would quickly start to develop – without being slowed down by salt – and there would not be sufficient time left for it to acquire a full flavor (and better structure) during the resting period. Therefore, yeast would also need to be added after the autolyse, not before.

When doughs are allowed proper resting times, adding fats is not usually necessary. Fat serves to make the bread more tender and keep longer. A proper resting time will provide the bread with these same qualities. However, in some cases you may want to add fat (e.g. butter or olive oil) for its flavor. In that case, it's important to know that adding fat encapsulates the strings of gluten formed in the dough, impeding them from gaining more length by making further connections. Thus, if you choose to add fats, they should be incorporated into the dough at the end of the second mixing or kneading – after autolyse and after mixing in salt and yeast.

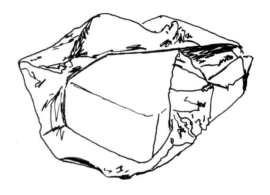

Spiral mixer

Equipment and kneading techniques

With regard to kneading techniques, the main thing to consider is that different tools have a different impact on the speed at which doughs develop and on the amount of oxidation taking place.

A planetary mixer

(such as a Hobart home mixing device) works very fast and should be handled with great care for a very brief amount of time – or avoided. These mixers do allow the flour to maintain its original qualities, because they prevent the dough from incorporating much oxygen. But the main drawback of this type of machine is that it works so intensively on the dough, at such high speed, that the dough quickly develops without the benefits of a slower process and more resting time.

Spiral mixers

work more slowly and give the gluten network a chance to

develop more at its own pace. However, they do incorporate more air into the dough, and using them for longer or at a higher speed than is strictly necessary causes the flour to lose flavor, color, and nutritive value.

A hand-held home mixer with dough hooks

works fine, especially on doughs which contain a lot of water. It works like a planetary mixer in many respects, and when used at a low speed, is not usually too aggressive. This type of mixer is not suitable for doughs which contain less water. These doughs usually tend to be stronger than the mixer, causing the mixer to overheat and bending the mixing hooks.

Hand kneading

is the most obvious technique to deploy when working at home with a normally hydrated dough. The chances of overworking a dough to the point of bleaching it are not very high. However, the same principles still apply: before autolyse only mix until the flour is hydrated, and after autolyse work the dough as little as possible, just until the salt and yeast are well mixed and evenly incorporated.

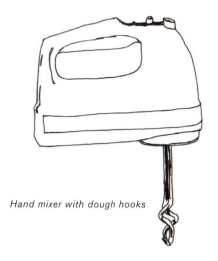

Hand mixer with dough hooks

Planetary mixer

63

Letting the dough rest and folding the dough

Photo: *The pizza bianca dough only starts to hold its shape after folding*

While the dough is resting

After mixing the ingredients and a period of autolyse the gluten network in the dough will already have started to develop. Still, it is not at its full, optimal strength. This process continues by simply letting the dough rest.

To be precise, the dough itself is not resting at all; several processes continue:

- The yeast, having been hydrated, has become active and starts to turn sugars into alcohol and carbon dioxide, the latter causing the dough to inflate.

- This inflation serves to stretch the gluten strands, and they in turn strengthen, just as if you were kneading the dough.

- The yeast's metabolism also causes the acidity in the dough to increase.

- Enzymes in the flour, most notably amylase, also become active the moment water and flour are mixed. Amylase breaks down the starch and turns it into various kinds of sugar.

- The sugar thus developed will in part be consumed again by the yeast, and in part stay in the dough contributing to its flavor and, while baking, to the development of the crust.

- In the case of a sourdough, bacteria start to produce all kinds of volatile organic acids, impacting both the flavor of the dough and its acidity. Even when not using sourdough, these processes start to take place, though at a much lower speed. Given enough time, a dough made with yeast will also become more acidic and develop more flavor.

- The increasing acidity of the dough serves both to strengthen the gluten strands and to break down the starch. The resulting bread will be more easily digestible and will keep fresh longer. However, this effect has its limits, and if the dough contains too much acidity the gluten network will start to break down.

- Finally, while resting, the flour continues absorbing water. Thus, the more resting time you allow, the more water you can use, without the dough becoming sticky and unworkable.

Simple rules

It's not feasible to quantify these processes – they depend on the characteristics of the flour, the circumstances under which the dough is made and kept, the temperature of the dough and the extent to which the dough has been worked during the mixing phase. Luckily, this is not necessary for present purposes nor to bake a high-quality bread. It is more important to be aware that these processes occur, and to develop experience and an intuitive awareness of what's happening to the dough.

To assist in this process, it's helpful to start out with some simple rules:

- The faster the yeast acts on the dough (e.g. due to a large quantity of yeast being added, or because the temperature of the dough is higher), the less time there will be for the process in which amylase turns starch into sugars. Even if you allow time, the sugars will in turn be consumed by the yeast. The flavor of the resulting bread will be bland, and the crust less "crusty" (less colorful, flavorful, and crisp).

- The more time you give a dough to develop, the more acids are produced and the more these in turn will work on the dough, making the bread more easily digestible, more flavorful, and longer lasting. It will also become increasingly chewy. The higher the level of acidity, the thicker the crust will generally be.

- The lower the temperature of a dough, the slower the processes will occur. The gluten will need more time to develop. The yeast's activity will slow down exponentially, the amylase will slow down, and, in particular, the sugars produced will not be directly consumed by the yeast.

- Finally, it's good to remember the importance of water. When there are more available water molecules in a dough – molecules which haven't yet physically or chemically attached to other molecules – most of the processes mentioned will go faster. Yeast, enzymes, bacteria all make use of the water that's available. Only the gluten networks will have a harder time developing when the dough is moister.

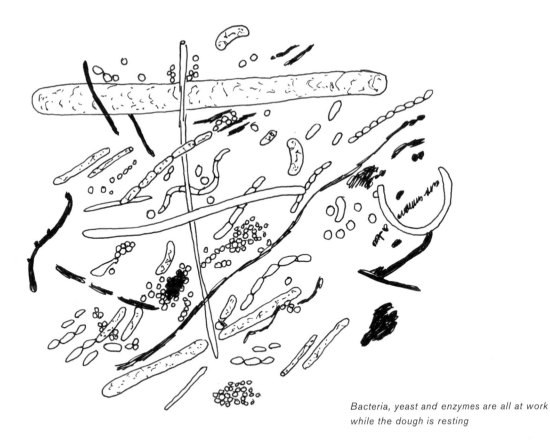

Bacteria, yeast and enzymes are all at work while the dough is resting

Gluten network before folding the dough, the gluten strands are shorter and randomly dispersed in all directions

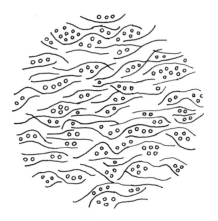

Gluten network after folding the dough, the gluten is lengthened and aligned

Folding the dough

While the dough rests, the gluten network continues to develop. However, the protein strings are dispersed in all directions. One simple act performed at the halfway point of the resting time can align the strands. This is the act of folding the dough. It's one of the most effective ways of kneading, in fact. With a few simple movements, gluten will be reinforced, aligned, and stretched, and you will instantly discover that even the loosest or stickiest of doughs turns into something smooth and strong. The inner and the outer parts of the dough are flipped or turned inside out; the temperature of the dough equalizes throughout. It also repositions the yeast and gives it access to a fresh supply of "food". The yeast's activity can then increase again, and it will no longer need to consume itself (it is this cannibalization which causes the typical flavor associated with too much yeast). Folding, moreover, is a very gentle act – there's hardly any oxidation or risk of overworking the dough.

Folding the dough

Take the dough out of its receptacle, place it on a work surface which is lightly floured or moistened with water, and flatten it slightly, without degassing it.

Pull the far side up and towards you, folding it about two thirds over the dough.

Then take the side closest to you and pull it away from you, again folding about two thirds over the dough.

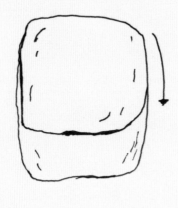

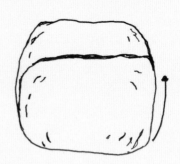

Do the same with the left side.

Then the right side.

Flatten the dough again slightly, and then repeat the process. Only this time you do not necessarily fold two-thirds, but up to the point you feel the dough can't be stretched further without tearing it, e.g. about halfway. Afterwards, put the dough back in its container and leave it to rest again.

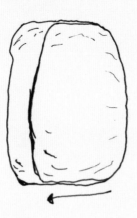

Folding causes the gluten strands to stretch to their maximum at the level of development at that moment. To leave the dough to rest again as we are doing gives the gluten a chance to relax. The strands will slowly become more extensible again. Shaping, the next step, will again involve stretching the gluten, and again aligning the strings of protein all into the same direction. But it is not possible to do this immediately after folding, as the dough will simply be more elastic rather than extensible, and tear easily. Normally, you fold at least one hour before shaping.

Depending on the nature of the dough, especially the amount of hydration reached, it is possible to repeat the process of folding several times (each time allowing a resting period in between), thus enabling very moist doughs to gain sufficient strength.

Ready?

The length of the total resting period depends on the recipe and the overall process you choose. You can vary between a shorter resting period before shaping (as long as the dough has developed adequately) and a long rest after shaping, or a longer resting period before shaping, and then start to bake more quickly. Very generally speaking, a dough should grow to more or less twice its original size, feel light and airy and still have some elasticity at the same time; it should be smooth to the touch, not sticky. The speed of dough development can be influenced by the temperature at which it rests: keeping dough in the fridge slows development down, maintaining it at room temperature speeds it up.

Shaping the dough

Shaping ("*façonnage*", in French, a term I will use a lot) is part of the fun of making bread. It is one of the more difficult parts to master. It requires developing a feel for the dough, working on your dexterity, making movements that are strong but at the same time subtle and careful. The way you shape a bread greatly impacts the internal structure of the loaf, its volume, and the cracking open of the crust into what the French call "*la grigne*", where the bread opens up while baking.

Unshaped loaves
In fact, the step of shaping a bread is optional. It is possible to move directly from resting to baking. The result would be less volume, a relatively flat final loaf and no distinct shape, but also a very nice open structure and full flavor if the resting period has been long enough. The bread would also be less crusty, that is, there would be a crust as with any other bread, but it would not be possible to make cuts in the bread and have a *grigne,* the part that actually provides the bread with its crusty bite after it is baked. Having said that, it is certainly worth a try, especially with more moist doughs; you could make a very high-quality ciabatta or focaccia, for instance.

The effects of shaping
Shaping acts on a dough in two main ways. It is a way of rearranging and strengthening the gluten networks so that the loaf has the desired shape and will hold this shape during further resting and eventually baking. It also puts tension on the dough, thus enabling it to burst open while baking (creating the *grigne* when cut properly before putting it in the oven) and expand in the desired way. Shaping using the appropriate techniques means you can leave the bread to have a long rest again before baking, enabling it to increase in volume even more and gain more flavor, while retaining its shape and strength.

Keeping this in mind, the main principle of shaping is not to just mold the bread into a certain shape, as if handling clay. It is to work the dough in such a way that the surface tension increases to the maximum, without tearing. As such, shaping is very similar to folding a dough.

Photo: pre-shaping stollen dough into balls

The main error that can happen when shaping is to degas the dough by handling it too firmly, thus pushing out all the air. The gas removed when pushing on the dough actually contains a lot of flavor: flavor which will be passed onto the crumb while baking. In the case of a sourdough loaf, pushing out the air will result in a more acidic-tasting bread. What happens is not that the bread becomes more acidic, but simply that the acidity is no longer balanced by the rich, volatile flavors contained in the gasses. The bread will simply become acidic but otherwise bland. Degassing the dough thus seriously compromises the flavor of the bread. However, if you wanted the bread to have a very regular structure without any larger alveoli, as you will see later is done for a classic *pain de mie*, pushing out the gas would be the right thing to do at this stage.

When making more than one loaf from a dough, the shaping process also involves weighing the pieces for each loaf. Cutting separates the mass of dough into individual pieces. The main thing here is to cut in a way which does as little harm as

possible to the internal structure of the dough. Make sharp, clean, straight cuts, without tearing or ripping the dough. Try not to touch the dough too much, as it will start to stick to your hands and eventually tear as well.

For professional bakers, this is the point where a difference can be made. Using a machine to weigh the dough causes the dough to degas and thus lose flavor. There are different tools and machines on the market, but all of them have, to a greater or lesser extent, a negative impact on the quality of the bread. If possible, weigh by hand. If this is not possible, choose a machine that puts minimal pressure on the dough pieces, and certainly avoid those that suck out all the air.

Pre-shaping and final shaping; techniques

Usually, in French baking, there are two stages of shaping: pre-shaping and final shaping. During the pre-shaping a very rough basic form is given to the bread, either a small roll or a ball-like shape, both carried out in a few simple movements done in such a way as to reach maximum tension. Then the dough is left to rest a little bit – depending on the elasticity of the gluten this could be anywhere from five to twenty minutes, the purpose of which is to let the gluten relax somewhat. After this, the bread is given its final shape, as gluten strands are once again stretched to their maximum, becoming ever stronger. After this final shape the bread has a last rest before baking.

Pre-shaping into a roll

To make a roll (the kind of pre-shaping suitable for a baguette, or a bread baked in a rectangular tin):

1. Cut the dough into rectangular pieces. Take one, fold the outer parts towards you, all the way, so that the seam is on the side of the dough piece, facing you.

2. Using your thumbs, push the seam underneath, not by turning the dough, but by stretching it. The upper part should remain on top throughout the process. It's like tucking in.

3. From the other side (the far side), almost from underneath, use flat hands to push the dough piece towards you. Your pinkies (little fingers) should be touching the dough, moving it across the working surface a bit. Use the resistance of the surface to pull in or tuck in the dough further, until you feel maximum tension has been reached on the surface of the dough. Again, the upper part of the dough should remain on top, the seam should remain underneath. Do not use too much flour, as this would just make the dough piece slide across the work surface rather than building the necessary tension.

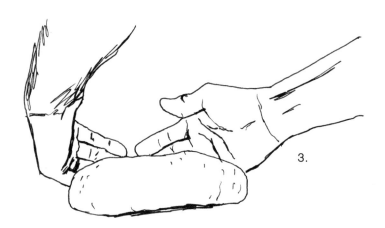

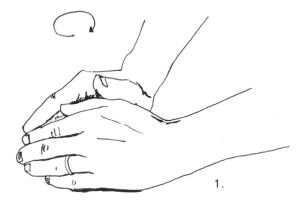

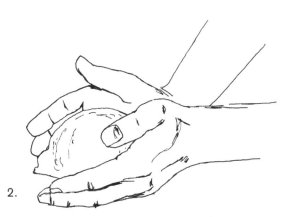

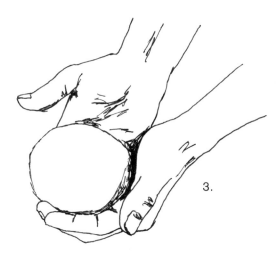

Pre-shaping into a ball

To make a ball (the pre-shaping suitable for a *boule* or round bread, but also for a *batard* or *fougasse*):

1. Place your hands on top of the dough piece and start to turn it swiftly on an unfloured work surface. Make sure you do not touch the dough too much (work quickly), so that it doesn't stick to your hands. Push a little bit while doing the first turn, so that the dough sticks to the work surface.

2. As soon as you feel it sticking, move your hands to the side of the dough, and keep on turning it, so it starts to build up tension.

3. Gradually move your fingers almost underneath the dough. During the process, the bottom of the dough piece should remain on the work surface and the top should remain on top. In fact, you are tucking in the dough piece in much the same way as when you were making the small roll, using the resistance of the work surface to build surface tension and reach a round shape. When making a ball, you want the work surface to be almost free of any flour.

Final shape: boule

The final shaping, of course, depends on which bread you are making.

The first main technique is to repeat the same shaping process on the pre-shaped ball, after a short rest, so its strength and shape are reinforced. You can do this in exactly the same way as when you pre-shaped it.

If you feel comfortable following the process above, you can also use the technique that is illustrated here:

1. Place the pre-shaped ball on the working surface with the seam on top (so upside down) and then flatten it just slightly.
2. Fold the outer parts inside, to the middle, one by one, creating a star shaped seam.
3. Turn the dough (so right side up) and shape it into a ball again in only two or three movements, making sure you reach maximum tension without entirely closing the seam. If, later when baking, you turn the dough piece again once more, with the seam up on a baking stone, and do not score it, the closure you made will open up again, making a beautiful star shaped *grigne*.

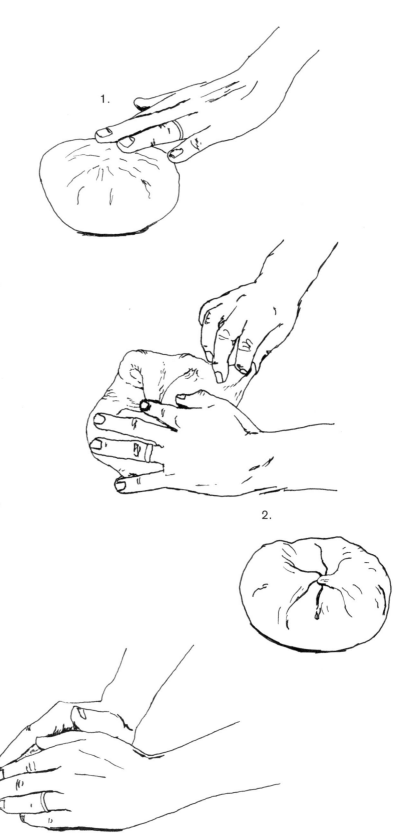

The other generally used technique is to either shape a roll into a baguette, or a ball into a *batard*.

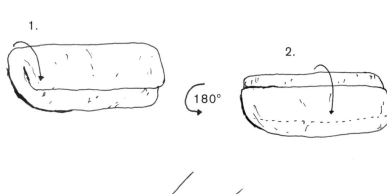

Final shape: baguette

To shape a roll into a baguette:

1. Place the roll in front of you with the seam upwards, then fold the outer part towards you until it covers about two thirds of the dough.
2. Turn the dough about 180 degrees (not upside down), then fold the outer part towards you until it again covers about two-thirds of the dough. Flatten slightly and gently, taking care not to push out the gases contained in the dough piece.

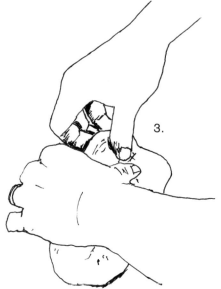

3. Fold the outer part towards you again, this time all the way (placing the thumb of one hand in the middle of the dough to fold around it and using the other hand to do the actual folding) so the seam will be at the side.
4. Close the seam with the palm of your hand, being careful to only close the seam, not to push air out of the rest of the dough.
5. Now push the seam underneath, without rolling the dough, creating more surface tension again.
6. Follow the same procedure as you did when pre-shaping into a roll.
7. Only this time, by using a slight pressure from above, even out the baguette and acquire the desired length.

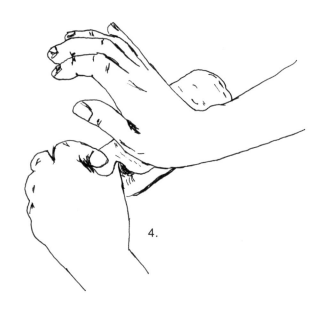

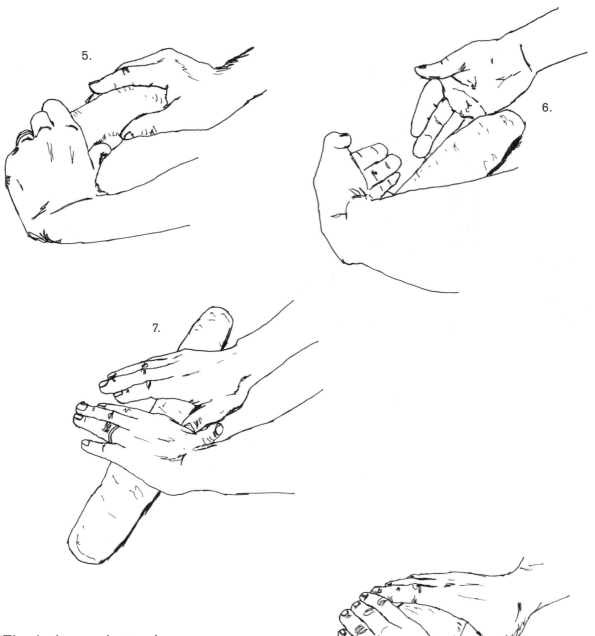

5.

6.

7.

Final shape: batard

To make a ball into a *batard*, follow exactly the same steps as when making a roll into a baguette (step 1 to 6), but be careful not to lose the original ball shape. The inner part should remain thicker, while ends of the dough piece are pointed.

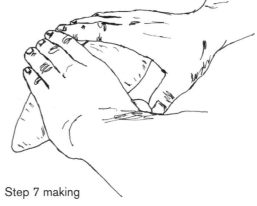

Step 7 making

a batard

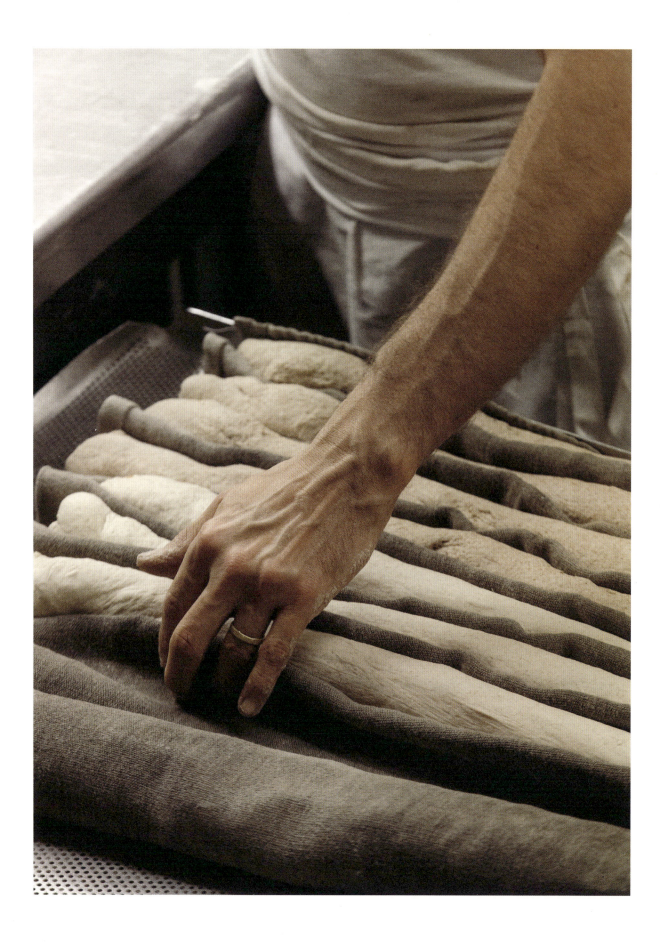

*Sourdough boules
in the proofing cabinet*

Continuing the resting phase

After shaping, repeat the resting phase, and all the processes taking place during this phase will continue once again. If you were to bake immediately, the bread would be too strong and unable to expand without breaking open; in fact, as the gluten has been tightened and cannot extend to contain more gases, the loaf would not expand at all while baking. Thus, another sufficient resting time is required. Very generally, the dough should feel airy again after this resting time and have increased in volume, but still be slightly resistant to the touch, still have some force left. When pushed, it should give a little, and then slowly regain its original shape.

The length of this resting phase depends on the nature of the dough and the temperature at which it rests. A dough which was already quite developed before shaping, or a dough which feels softer due to high level of hydration or a "weak" flour, could be ready for baking in as little as half an hour. If you put the unbaked loaves in a cold place, such as a fridge, or in a proofing cabinet with a low temperature, it is possible to extend this phase to up to 30 hours with excellent results.

Planning resting times; working with the fridge

There are two approaches to letting the dough rest: working your way around a fixed, inflexible schedule of dough development; or allowing the dough to adapt to exactly to what works for it. Of course, the latter is utopia, but you can get surprisingly close to it. Once you become more skillful and acquire an intuition for the speed at which a dough develops, you can slow it down or speed it up along the way.

Part of this starts by choosing the initial dough temperature. If you want the dough to have a long time to rise – the primary fermentation – starting it for instance in the morning before going to work and planning to shape the loaves in the evening after you get back home again, you might use relatively cold water and then place the dough in the fridge just after mixing. When you come home, it does not matter exactly when you start working on it again – the fridge will slow the dough development down in such a way that an hour or even a few hours make little difference. You might start immediately, and then leave the shaped loaves at room temperature, so you can bake them later in the evening. Or you might put them back in the fridge and bake early the next morning. You could put the shaped loaves back into the fridge immediately, if you feel the dough is developing quickly, or after some time, if it seems to be slow, in fact compensating for a relative lack of predevelopment by giving an extra impetus to the proofing or second rise. This is just an example, of course, in fact there are infinite ways to plan your timing around making bread, as long as you keep an eye on what's happening and understand which factors to take into account.

Another way of planning, which is similar to what we do in our bakery, is to do *façonnage* a few hours after making the dough. After mixing the ingredients, you place the dough in the fridge (or in a cold proofing cabinet) and then, depending on how much the dough has developed, put it straight back in the fridge again after shaping, or leave it at room temperature for a bit first (even five minutes or half an hour could have a considerable impact). At home, something like this could work: make the dough right after coming home from work, in the late afternoon or early evening, fold it just after dinner and take a few minutes to shape it just before going to bed. Leave the dough in the fridge overnight and then bake the next morning when you wake up.

The nice thing is that a dough with relatively little yeast, kept at colder temperatures, also becomes somewhat more tolerant; just as adding a *poolish* or *biga* (see pages 100-101) might also help to obtain consistent results even when conditions vary. With sourdough, you have a similar margin, but you should realize that the dough might become too sour if kept too long.

Baking

At this point, your loaf is ready to be baked. Again, you have a variety of choices: baking on a baking stone, on a baking tray, in a Dutch oven, or in a tin makes for completely different bread.

Stone baking

In French baking, and traditionally in many places around the world, the most common choice is to use an oven with a floor made of stone, and to bake directly on its surface. It is indispensable for the formation of a proper crust, for the *grigne* on a baguette, for full flavor and for the open and slightly irregular inner structure of French bread. The direct transfer of heat triggered by putting the dough directly on the hot stone floor leads to an explosion in the dough, causing it to rapidly expand in volume within a few minutes. A crust starts to form, and then, while the bread rises dramatically, the crust will burst open at its weakest spot, where the baker has used a razor to make a very fine and delicate incision, thus opening the *grigne*. The transfer of heat will gradually slow down, as the stone has passed on its initial warmth to the bread, so you can leave the bread in the oven longer to bake more slowly until it is well baked, has reached its full flavor and formed a well-developed crust.

You can read more about cutting the bread and obtaining the grigne in the appendix on page 233

For those baking at home without a stone oven, it is actually possible to simulate, or at least approximate, the exact same circumstances in any domestic oven. The trick is to place an unglazed tile in the oven and preheat to the maximum. These are the same tiles used for floors or patios, and are usually available from gardening centers or the like. Once the stone is preheated, you can bake directly on it in the oven. As the volume and weight of the breads you will be baking at one time at home are less than those a baker would bake, it actually doesn't matter that the stone and the oven is smaller than those of a professional baker, as long as the proportions are right. For professional bakers who would like to bake real French bread the only obvious choice would be to acquire a good stone oven.

Another important element of baking bread is allowing for the proper humidity in the oven, especially at the initial stages of baking. Steam in the oven helps transfer heat more directly to

the loaf than does air. The steam also helps to keep the crust moist, allowing it to expand much more than would be possible in a dry environment. Too much steam, however, makes the crust so flexible that it will not burst open and there will be no *grigne*. Finally, numerous chemical reactions take place on the crust of the bread, which depend on the availability of moisture. These are the reactions – most notably between proteins and sugars – which give a rich color to the crust and are in large part responsible for the bread's characteristic flavor. Moreover, as long as you resist the urge to slice the bread until it is completely cooled, the flavors developed in the crust are transferred to the crumb as the bread cools. With no steam, or insufficient steam, bread remains dull and bland, however well developed the original dough.

Towards the end of baking, on the other hand, the air in the oven should become dry, enabling the crust to finally set, and become "crusty". Keeping steam in the oven until the end of baking will lead to a very thick, tough crust.

While in a professional oven one push of a button is enough to open a valve to blow steam of about 430°F to 480°F (220°C to 250°C) directly into the oven, at home it will be slightly more laborious. Here are a few tricks developed by home bakers which work remarkably well.

- Spray the oven walls with water using a plant mister just before and especially immediately after putting in the bread. Be sure to quickly close the oven door. When using a mister, do not spray directly onto the bread. This would cause the bread to cool down, rather than assist in the immediate transfer of heat.

- An easier, similarly effective trick is to place a baking tray at the bottom of the oven while preheating. Immediately after putting the bread in the oven, pour some boiling water into the additional tray. The quantity of water should be such that it will immediately start to cause steam, but will completely evaporate within eight to fifteen minutes, depending on the size of the loaves (the bigger they are, the longer the steam is needed). Both tricks can also be combined. Whichever you choose, remember that steam is very hot! Preferably use gloves while pouring in water and keep your face at a safe distance.

A last note with regard to baking in domestic ovens: too much ventilation causes the bread to dry out. So, if you have a choice, turn off the ventilation while the bread is in the oven, or turn it on and off intermittently if it's needed to maintain sufficient heat. Ventilation in most domestic ovens is fortunately not that strong anyway. The ovens to avoid are professional kitchen ovens such as those used in many restaurants. These sometimes have such a strong fan that the crust will not stay humid long enough, causing the bread to remain small in volume, acquire both a bland color and bland flavor, and burst open very irregularly or not at all.

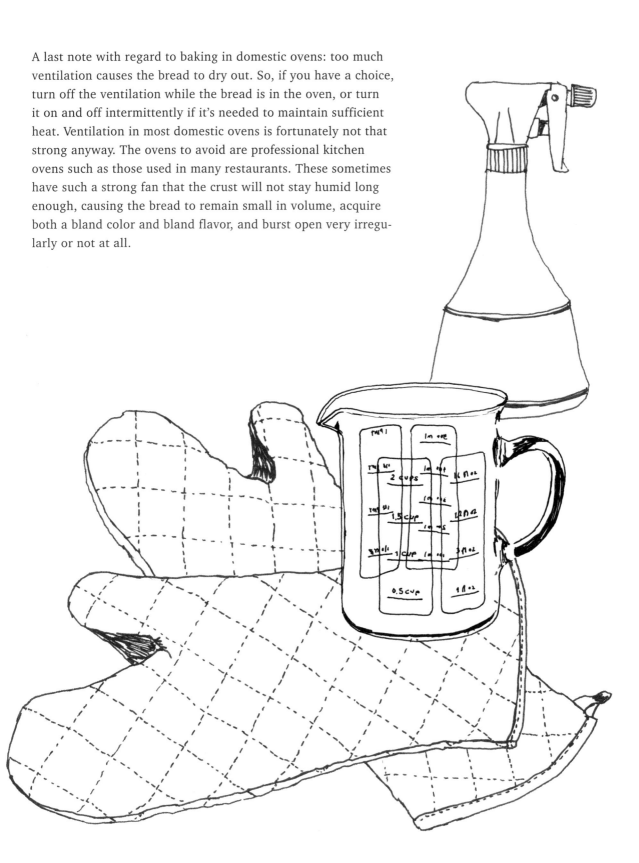

On a baking tray or in a baking tin

As any attentive reader will have noted, my preference is for bread with a well-developed crust. However, in some cases, as with *stollen*, for instance, you might want the crust to be finer or thinner instead of crunchy, and the inner structure of the bread to be finer as well. The French would call this a *pain de mie*, a "bread of the crumb". This is not difficult to achieve. The main concern when baking is to protect the bread from the direct transfer of heat associated with a stone oven. This can be done in two ways: by using a baking tray (either placed on the stone in a stone oven, or on a rack of an ordinary oven) or by using baking tins. A baking tray would be suitable for bread

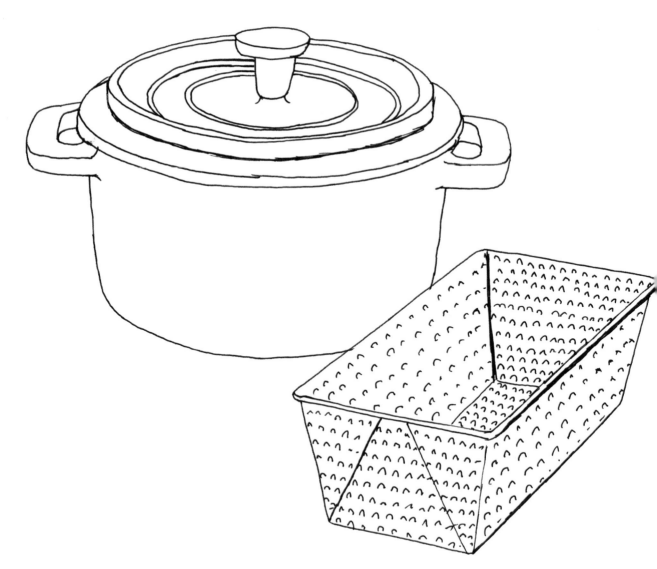

baked without a mould, and a baking tin suitable for a cake-shaped bread. A tin with a lid has a further advantage as no steaming is required, since the moisture in the bread cannot escape.

In a Dutch oven

Baking in a Dutch oven is a good trick for making a crusty round loaf without placing a stone in your oven and without steaming. Here you want an especially solid Dutch oven fitted with a lid. Preheating the Dutch oven ensures the direct transfer of heat needed. Closing the lid maintains the proper level of humidity and protects the bread from an oven fan. You may choose to remove the lid towards the end of baking, so that the crust starts drying out and becomes crisp.

To bake bread in a Dutch oven, first prepare either a shaped round loaf ready for baking, or use unshaped dough at the desired level of development. Place the empty Dutch oven in the oven and preheat. When preheated, use oven mitts to remove the hot Dutch oven from the oven and quickly put the bread in, upside down. Immediately replace the lid and return it to the hot oven.

This method for baking "unshaped" bread became world famous as the so-called "no knead bread" after Jim Lahey, a New York baker, posted a video on the internet.

Creating and maintaining a sourdough culture

If you haven't baked much yet, you may want to start off using commercial yeast. When you are ready to take it one step further, making your own sourdough opens up a new pallet of flavors. Sourdough is not very complicated to make, but it requires some discipline, as well as developing a knack for the process. The discipline involves an initial investment of a few minutes every day to start and refresh the sourdough. Once established, the sourdough requires maintenance every three days. It's very much like watering plants – it ultimately comes down to consistency of effort.

Having decided to go for it, this is what you should do to start.

<u>Day 1</u>

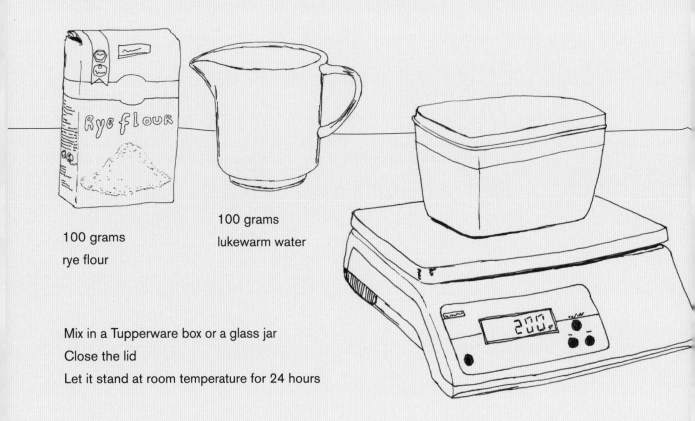

100 grams
rye flour

100 grams
lukewarm water

Mix in a Tupperware box or a glass jar
Close the lid
Let it stand at room temperature for 24 hours

Day 2

Discard half of the mixture

Then add to the remaining half:

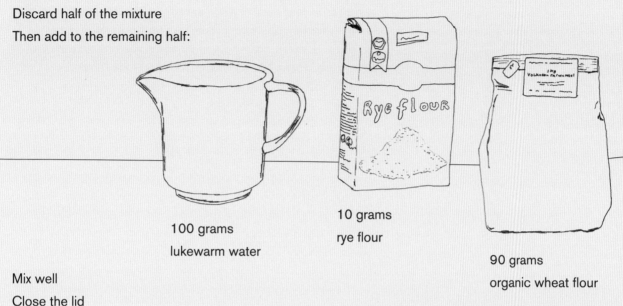

100 grams
lukewarm water

10 grams
rye flour

90 grams
organic wheat flour

Mix well

Close the lid

Let it stand at room temperature for 24 hours

Day 3 till ± day 7

Discard all but 100 grams of the mixture

Then add to the remaining 100 grams:

100 grams lukewarm water

10 grams rye flour

90 grams organic wheat flour

Mix well

Close the lid

Let it stand at room temperature for 24 hours

Repeat the same steps every day until the mixture
becomes very bubbly. When at its full strength the
mixture will double in volume after being left to stand
for a day. It will taste slightly acidic and alcoholic.
Usually, this will take about a week in total.

You now have a ready-to-use sourdough, and you might like to increase the quantity, if you want to start baking bread with it. Do not discard any of the mixture and keep roughly the same proportions when refreshing: one part of the old mixture should be refreshed with one part flour (10% rye) and one part water. When you use the sourdough to bake, always be sure to save some of it to start off the next batch.

Maintaining the sourdough

To maintain an active sourdough, it is not necessary to refresh it daily. Rather, after refreshing, leave it at room temperature for one or two hours, until it just starts becoming bubbly again. Transfer it to the fridge for up to three days. This process allows the sourdough to reach its full development slowly. The sourdough should be completely bubbly and active the day following refreshing, at which time you could use it to bake, incorporating it into the rest of your dough directly from the fridge. You can continue to use the sourdough without refreshing it for a further two days. At some point, you will see that the sourdough starts becoming less active and more liquid. This means it has passed its maturity and should be refreshed immediately.

The exact timing and speed of this process is difficult to predict, but after a while, you will get a feeling for just how long you should leave the sourdough out of the fridge after refreshing it, and for when it is ready for use (very bubbly, increased volume, more liquid but still strong enough, acidic but not too acidic). And the good thing is, the fridge slows down the process, extending the time when the sourdough is at its best and thereby allowing for some margin of error. If you bake when the sourdough is not yet active enough or is no longer active, the bread will take more time to develop, becoming slightly sour. But it can still be very nice. If you keep the sourdough too long in the fridge before refreshing it, the first refresh might not be as good, but you could leave it out at room temperature a bit longer, then put in the fridge again and refresh it again the next day, thus reactivating the sourdough.

Photo: Anna divides the newly refreshed sourdough

Things to avoid

Issues to avoid are: remnants of soap in the receptacle containing the freshly made sourdough, or contamination by other bacteria because of using dirty equipment or not taking proper care. A sourdough, especially when active, has a lot of resistance, because the bacteria present in it will out-compete new species, but, when being refreshed, it is vulnerable because it is considerably diluted. Also avoid keeping the sourdough so long that the acidity produced by the bacteria and yeast starts to break down the gluten, and the dough becomes watery. Finally, never put the sourdough directly in the fridge after a refreshment. The natural yeasts and bacteria present will not have a proper chance to recuperate and start growing again in quantity. The yeast in particular will not be able to regain its proper activity.

Now that you know the basics, and have created your own sourdough, there are a few things to understand and keep in mind, so you can make appropriate choices to suit your purposes.

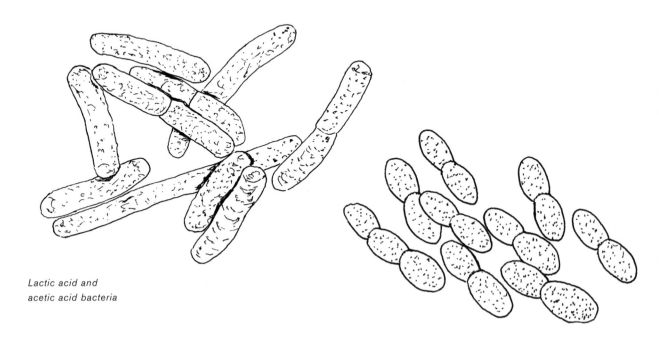

Lactic acid and acetic acid bacteria

Sourdough and temperature

Sourdough is a mixture of natural yeasts, which are slightly more resistant to acidity than commercially available yeast, and bacteria. The combination produces acidity, which makes the bread more easily digestible and enables it to stay fresh longer, alongside a very rich assortment of volatile organic acids that add flavor to the dough. Temperature influences the balance between yeast and bacteria. Yeast is at its best between 75°F to 95°F (24°C to 35°C) – this is why a newly refreshed sourdough should be kept at room temperature for some time before being placed in the fridge. Storing sourdough at a very low temperature also negatively affects the development, survival, and activity of bacteria. Thus, when putting the sourdough in the fridge, make sure the fridge is not too cold and choose a relatively warm spot inside the fridge. If you keep the sourdough at an external temperature of around 46°F (8°C), the temperature of the dough itself will be a few degrees warmer because of the heat produced by its internal activity, at around 52°F or 54°F (11°C or 12°C) is ideal. At a lower temperature, some species of bacteria will not be able to compete, even though the yeast will survive, resulting in a bland flavor.

Liquid and firm sourdough

The level of liquidity of a sourdough has a strong impact on its nature. A more moist and airy environment benefits bacteria which produce lactic acids, while a more solid, dry environment benefits anaerobic bacteria which produce acetic acid, like vinegar. Thus, choosing a liquid sourdough, as we have done, will result in bread with a much lighter, mild flavor. Depending on the process used, a liquid sourdough of this type may contain just a slight hint of acidity, but still maintains a very full flavor. Making your sourdough more solid will result in a distinctively sour bread. Watch out – if you aren't careful (especially when extending the development time of the bread to more than 16-18 hours), a more solid sourdough will produce a bread with the strong flavor of vinegar. Both types of bread can be very nice when made with care.

The liquidity of the sourdough also has an impact on the structure of the bread: a runnier sourdough helps to create an open airy structure of the bread, by affecting the qualities of the gluten being formed.

To make a firm sourdough starter

To get a more solid sourdough, simply change the proportion when refreshing to two parts flour and one part water and knead by hand rather than with a kitchen mixer (or use a planetary mixer).

Consequences of using more or less sourdough; adding yeast to a sourdough

When baking with sourdough, you can add more or less of it to a dough. Using too much will result in a weaker dough, as the acidity of the sourdough will weaken the gluten strands. After keeping the dough for some time, the gluten strands may actually break completely. Excessive proportions of sourdough also cause the flavor of the bread to be dominated by the sourdough, with the crust bland and lacking bite because the sourdough consumes sugars in the dough. On the other hand, using too little sourdough results in a bread developing too slowly, producing an acidic, dense loaf with a relatively bland crust. Depending on the strength of your sourdough (it should be fully developed, alive, and bubbly when liquid) you can still vary the quantity a bit, and judge the results for yourself. In general, to achieve the open structure of French bread and a very mildly sour flavor, add between one quarter and one half of the weight of the flour in the dough (e.g. when using 1000 grams of flour, you would add between 250 and 500 grams of sourdough).

As I mentioned earlier, many bakers add commercial yeast to their sourdough, without informing their customers. In principle, there's nothing wrong with this, as long as they inform their clientele. It is just another way of making bread and ensuring consistency on a day-to-day basis. It makes for speedy development, while enhancing the qualities of the sourdough in the final bread, giving it a stronger, more pronounced flavor and longer shelf life. It is just important to realize that it is not necessary to add yeast to sourdough, but a choice. A well-developed sourdough produces a very high quality of bread and very reliable development even without yeast. And, if you want to take advantage of extended development, commercial yeast will not work in the sourdough. It will be overpowered by the natural yeast present in the sourdough which is more suited to its slightly acidic environment.

Choice of flour

The use of different types of flours also has a strong impact on the sourdough. For the sourdough recipe in this book, we started out by using – preferably organic – rye flour, because it normally contains both a lot of bacteria and natural yeasts, as well as plenty of nutrients for the bacteria and yeast to feed on. However, if we were to continue using only rye flour for the refreshments, the sourdough would remain dense (as rye flour does not have the capacity to form gluten), become very acidic, and have very little strength. There would be literally too many nutrients available for the bacteria, and the natural yeast would suffer from the acidity. Making a wholemeal sourdough would have similar consequences, though to a lesser extent. Organic white flour (type 55 or 65) is thus most suitable for creating a strong, active sourdough, without it becoming too acidic. The addition of a small proportion of rye flour helps to provide sufficient nutrients.

Working with a yeast starter dough

(poolish, biga, pâte fermentée)

Poolish, biga, or *pâte fermentée* are all different kinds of starters based on yeast: small amounts of dough made in advance, to be added to the main dough after they have already undergone initial fermentation.

In a bakery, or at home, using a starter allows you to shorten the development time of the final dough, while adding the characteristics of the starter dough, such as increased acidity and flavor development. The specific effects depend very much on the kind of starter used. As with sourdough, a firm starter, such as a *biga*, has a different impact than a more hydrated starter, such as a *poolish*. In a *biga*, the firm starter, development of the dough slows due to lack of water, leading to increased acidity, and, as with a sourdough, to the development of anaerobic bacteria producing acetic acids (though not to the same extent as in a sourdough). Often a *biga* will develop for a full day or more before being incorporated into a final bread dough.

A more liquid starter, such as a *poolish*, will develop much more quickly and could be made as little as a few hours ahead of time if necessary. Breads that incorporate a poolish will have a more aerated structure and a much milder acidic flavor. Also, the gluten in the poolish will be more extensible in nature than those in the *biga*. The bread made from a poolish thus may have a slightly larger volume, and particularly the alveoli in the bread will be more pronounced. In the end, the preference for *biga* or poolish is mainly a matter of taste, resting on slight, though certainly discernible, differences. Many traditional recipes either call for one or the other starter, with some variance according to region of origin. The *biga* is typically used in Italian baking, the poolish much more frequently in France, both for baguettes and for *"pain de campagne"*, country bread.

Use of a starter offers many advantages to bakers. Foremost among them is that the baker can bring the starter to a level of dough development which would not be possible to achieve in a bread made in one step (a direct dough). If you were to leave the whole dough to develop overnight at room temperature, for instance, it might develop too much. In that case the gluten strands will not have any force anymore, stretching to the point that they cannot contain more gases, and collapsing during baking. Furthermore, the sugars present and formed in the dough would be consumed by the yeast, and thus flavor would become bland and the crust pale and weak. Thus, using a starter is a way to give the dough a very full flavor, while retaining a strong dough containing sufficient sugars for a good crust.

Another alternative starter would be a *pâte fermentée*, which is basically a piece of pre-fermented dough. While poolish and *biga* are made without salt, consisting of flour, water, and a little yeast, *pâte fermentée* contains salt, which makes the starter consistency the same as that of the final dough. Gluten strands will be a bit tighter, as the salt inhibits their extensibility, and development will be slowed down by the salt. Thus, the amount of yeast in the *pâte fermentée* must be higher than in a poolish or *biga*. I prefer poolish and *biga* because of their more pronounced qualities, but some traditional recipes you may come across do call for this kind of starter. Traditionally, the main reason for the popularity of the *pâte fermentée* was that a piece of dough left over from one day's baking would be saved to add to a new dough on the next.

In all cases when working with starters, you replace part of the final dough with the chosen starter. Accordingly, depending on the consistency of the starter, you will add less water, flour, or salt to the final dough. When working with a poolish or *biga,* you might not need to add any yeast at all to the final dough, if the starter is already powerful enough. An exception to this rule is the case of very rich doughs containing a lot of butter, sugar, milk, or eggs, as these ingredients can slow down the development of the dough and call for a higher percentage of yeast.

The amount of pre-fermented dough you use as starter is again a matter of choice – there are no fixed rules. Just experiment to find out what works best.

Using percentages

Please note that flour in the USA and Canada is often stronger when compared to European flour. This means that you may need to add considerably more water to the dough to reach a specified consistency. A difference of 10% would not be unlikely.

In professional bakeries, it is common to record recipes in percentages rather than grams or ounces. The convention has a practical purpose, as quantities may be adjusted daily, to meet the demand of the changing flow of customers and the always varying orders for bread by restaurants. But it also helps those new to baking to develop an understanding of the recipe.

Seeing ingredients presented as percentages makes it easier to compare different recipes, to understand their basic makeup at a single glance. For instance, a recipe specifying a dough has "50% water" indicates that the bread will be quite strong and dry; 60% that it will be very average, 70% or more that it will be quite hydrated and soft.

These percentages are always expressed in relation to the total weight of flour present in the dough. Thus, 50% water means, for instance, 500 grams water to 1000 grams flour. 2% salt means 20 grams of salt would go into the same dough, and 1% of yeast stands for 10 grams. Adding twice as much flour, i.e. making a dough with 2000 grams flour, would mean all these amounts are changed accordingly. Sometimes different flours are mixed together, in that case, 80% wheat and 20% rye flour, for instance, would mean 800 grams of wheat and 200 grams of rye, adding up to a total of 1 kg, or 100%.

Apart from helping to understand the qualities of the dough, compare different recipes, and easily adjust the quantities, these percentages have the advantage of making it easy to adjust recipes to your preferences. If a particular flour appears to absorb a bit more water, it is easy to adjust the water percentage a little, e.g. going from 60% to 62%, to achieve the required level of hydration.

Photo: liquid sourdough is added to make a batard dough

How to use
the recipes

Recipes are formulas. They are little experiments, written down in code. Formulas need to be read, and the riddles in the code need to be solved. This section provides you with the keys to understanding the recipes – how they are structured and how to read them – but also how to foresee from the formula what its outcome will be and how to repeat the experiments. In other words, how to prevent the dough from becoming sticky all over, when to use a dough hook or mixer and when not, and how to make sure it's you rather than the dough who decides the work schedule.

Ingredients

The recipes in this book are all structured in a similar way. First there is the list of ingredients, shown both in quantities (e.g. 1 kilo of flour) and in percentages, with all ingredients measured in relation to the weight of the flour (e.g. 2% salt indicating twenty grams of salt to one kilo or 1000 grams of flour). This already gives you an indication of the kind of dough you will be working with. The hydration level will tell you whether you will be making a moister, softer dough, or a drier, stronger dough. The amount of yeast or sourdough used will give you an indication of the speed at which the dough will develop, the flavor that will be obtained, and whether it might be good to leave the dough at room temperature or to place it in the fridge to slow development.

With regard to the baguette recipes where the weight of the breads will depend on your own preferences and the size of your oven, I have chosen to work with one kilo of flour. This makes it easier to immediately understand the differences between the recipes in case the percentages still seem a bit abstract. Of course, you can adjust the recipe in line with the number of breads you would like to make.

Often, the amounts are indicated with a margin – depending on the qualities of the flour, on the time available, on the temperature at which you work, you might for instance choose to add a bit more or less yeast, or more or less water. This is really something you will have to find out and optimize for yourself, adjusting the recipe to the ingredients, the circumstances, and your schedule.

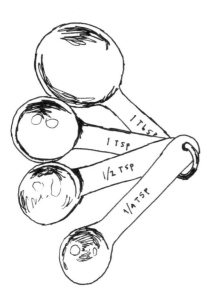

When starting off you can simply use the midpoint of the range indicated in the recipe. For instance, if the recipe indicates 630 to 680 grams of water, take 650 grams. A more hydrated dough is a little more difficult to work with, so if shaping is still an issue you could also choose to use the lower margin and work with 630 grams of water.

When comparing these recipes with other recipes in other books, remember that we specify the amount of instant yeast to be used. If you are using fresh yeast, you would need three times as much. Thus 0.67% of yeast in our recipes would be equivalent to 2% in a recipe calling for fresh yeast.

The ideal type of flour per recipe is also specified. If it isn't available, feel free to use any other kind of flour. You might have to adjust the water percentage, however, as different types of flour might absorb more or less water.

Measuring small amounts of yeast and salt

Often the recipes require very small amounts of yeast and salt. This can be quite tricky with ordinary kitchen scales – a set of measuring spoons is much more precise. Of course, this also depends on the type of salt you are using. The more coarsely ground the salt, the lighter weight it will contain for a fixed volume. So, it is worth checking the first time with a tablespoon, and then, if necessary, make some adjustments based on your particular salt.

Keep in mind: In a professional bakery, legal standards might apply to the salt percentage allowed in bread. For the recipes in this book, we are using the original percentages as used to be common in France, percentages that are well suited to home baking and result in flavorful, yet not overly salty, bread.

	tablespoon	teaspoon	½ teaspoon	¼ teaspoon
salt	20 g	6.7 g	3.3 g	1.7 g
yeast	14 g	4.7 g	2.3 g	1.2 g

Mixing

Each recipe indicates whether or not the autolyse technique is to be used (the short resting phase before mixing in salt and yeast), as well as whether and for how long the dough is kneaded. When making a dough, either you mix in all ingredients at once, or you start with just flour and water, mix them until the flour is hydrated, leave it to stand, and then mix or knead in salt and yeast, again just until well incorporated and evenly distributed. This stage is only followed by a more or less intense period of kneading in certain cases. When using oil or fats, they are usually added at the final stage of mixing or kneading, to avoid the fats interacting with the process of gluten formation at too early a stage.

To mix flour and water it is easiest to use a big, round, mixing bowl, and proceed by hand. When working with a very moist dough, you might want to use a hand mixer with dough hooks, at a low speed. It could also be more convenient not to use a round bowl in this case, but a rectangular Tupperware box. In a rectangular container it will be easier to incorporate all the flour, or to work the dough more strongly if needed, by moving the mixer back and forth, almost in a kneading motion. Sometimes you will find that mixing is easier if you start off with the water, and then add the flour to it.

If the dough sticks too much to your hands, keep your hands slightly moist, rather than using flour to prevent sticking. This will prevent you from kneading in more and more flour. When mixing in salt and yeast, proceed in a similar fashion as the first step, again working either by hand or with a hand mixer. Pay attention to how you add the salt and yeast though – never at the same time, to avoid direct contact. Add the two ingredients one after the other, sprinkling them finely over the dough to avoid lumps and encourage them to incorporate more easily – lumps of instant yeast are especially hard to dissolve later on.

Finally, adding fats can also be done either by hand or with a hand mixer. When using butter, make sure it is not too cold, so it can be easily incorporated. It is possible to make both more moist or more dry doughs with a professional mixer. However, when adding butter to a dough, it is better to first mix by hand. Otherwise, the butter can stick to the edges of the bowl and take much more time to be incorporated fully, thus increasing the necessary mixing time, and compromising the quality of the dough.

Temperature

Each recipe provides a temperature recommendation, indicating the optimal dough temperature after mixing ingredients and – if called for – kneading. Of course, you can only measure the dough temperature after you have made the dough, at which point it is too late to make alterations. But it provides a valuable indication that tells you how to adjust next time. The temperature also indicates whether you might want to put the dough directly in the fridge (or even in the freezer for a bit) to cool it down quickly if it is too warm, or on the other hand leave it out at room temperature for some time if it is too cold. To get to a dough temperature of, for instance, 75°F (24°C), you might want to use water that is slightly warmer, e.g. 81°F (27°C) when making a dough that is not worked too much. When making a dough that is worked a lot, you will need to use colder water, as the temperature of the dough increases as it is worked. To obtain a temperature of, for instance, 54°F (12°C) or colder, you might need to use ice water, as the other ingredients will be at room temperature, and you will need to compensate for their warming effect.

It is also possible to make a calculation in advance, taking into account variables like the kind of mixing equipment used, the weight of a mixing bowl, and the number of minutes that the dough is needed. I would not advise taking it this far at home, and it is not really necessary even in an artisan bakery either.

You can use any dough or kitchen thermometer

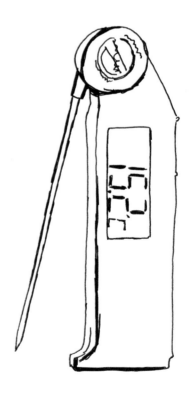

Resting times / dough fermentation and development

After mixing, all doughs have one or more resting phases to allow them to develop and increase in volume. Usually, one before *façonnage* (weighing and shaping the loaves), called the primary fermentation, and one after *façonnage*, called secondary fermentation or proofing. Depending on the recipe, but also on your own schedule, resting can be done either in the fridge or at room temperature. In both cases you want to prevent the dough from drying out. The easiest and best way during the first resting phase is usually to cover the bowl or container in which you keep the dough with a piece of plastic film. An alternative method, but not one suitable for keeping the dough for a longer time, is to cover the bowl with a damp dishtowel.

To prevent the dough from sticking to the container or bowl, causing it to tear when removed – and thus damaging its internal structure – it is best to lightly oil the container before putting in the dough. Flour can also be used for this purpose but, especially if the dough is to be kept for a longer time, it may not prove adequate and will just be absorbed by the dough.

The resting times indicated in the recipes often have a large margin when the dough is kept under refrigeration. Because the dough will develop very slowly at colder temperatures a lot of flexibility is allowed for and decisions mostly depend on your own planning. For instance, if you know in advance that you want to go for the longest possible time for the primary fermentation, then work towards a slightly lower dough temperature; if you would like the proofing to be prolonged, then place the dough pieces directly back in the fridge after shaping to keep cool, etc.

When working with long and cold proofing, and if the dough is not developing sufficiently, you may also keep it at room temperature for a short time after shaping and before placing it back in the fridge – as little as fifteen minutes to one hour can even have an impact. If you find you have been on the careful side and you suspect that the bread is not sufficiently developed before baking, you can also take the bread out of the refrigerator a couple of hours before baking to adjust for that and speed up its development.

Finally, when leaving the bread to develop for a long time it never hurts to check midway in the process how the bread is doing. If your fridge is on the warm side, or if your dough was already quite developed before refrigerating, the bread might be developing faster than expected. You can then bake the bread sooner than planned, and for the next time, adjust the dough temperature.

Folding the dough

In between resting, many of the recipes call for the dough to be folded or be given a "turn" (a "*rabat*" in French). This is done on a work surface. If you are working with a dry dough, you could sprinkle a very thin layer of flour onto the work surface, and keep your hands floured as well. When working with a moist dough, you can make the surface slightly moist and keep your hands slightly moist, or, in the case of, for instance, *pizza bianca*, use a lot of flour. Be careful not to incorporate the flour into the inside of the dough: the dough will become slightly drier as a result. But also, there will be bits of under-developed flour inside the bread, and these bits will dry out much more quickly after baking. In all cases, the more quickly you work and the more lightly you handle the dough, the less flour or water you will need, simply because you don't give it the time to become sticky.

Façonnage

Façonnage or shaping the bread begins with weighing out the dough pieces for individual loaves from the whole dough. To do so, remove the dough from its container and transfer it to a lightly floured work surface. Use a dough cutter, which is a piece of plastic with a sharp edge. If a dough cutter is not available, a big kitchen knife with a flat blade will do. Cut the dough by pressing the cutter through the dough and immediately pulling away the dough piece before it starts sticking to the rest of the dough again. Don't slice back and forth as you would normally do with a knife. Weigh the dough piece. If it is too heavy, remove some of it using the cutter. If it is not big enough, cut and add another small dough piece. Working quickly with a light touch will prevent the dough from sticking to the scales or to your hands. If making multiple loaves, you normally first weigh all the pieces of dough, before starting the shaping.

The recipes provide an indication of the shape you want to achieve in the pre-shaping step or *pré-façonnage* (usually a roll or ball) and of the final shape you want to obtain (e.g. a baguette, *batard* or *boule*). In between shaping and pre-shaping you leave the dough pieces to rest for a bit, so the gluten can relax. Place the dough pieces on a very lightly floured surface to prevent sticking, and cover them loosely with a piece of plastic (not plastic film, as this would attach itself to the dough, but for example, a cut-open plastic bag placed loosely on top). You can see how the different pre-shapes and shapes are obtained in the section about shaping on pages 72-81.

After shaping, place the dough inside a plastic bag on a lightly floured *couche* (a dishtowel on a baking tray might do the trick – see page 229) and leave it to rest again at room temperature or in the fridge. This is the proofing stage.

Baking

Then, finally, it is time to bake the bread. Pay special attention to whether the bread should be baked on a baking stone, in a tin, a Dutch oven, or on a baking tray, and whether you have to create steam or not (on pages 86-89 you can find how to go about creating steam in a home oven). Make sure the oven has been preheated adequately. Scoring the bread to obtain a *grigne* (see page 216), is normally done just before baking, when the dough is already on a dough peel or a baking tray. Instructions on how to make a peel and place the loaves on it are on page 230.

The oven temperatures listed in the recipes are always only indications. Carefully watch what happens and adjust the temperature accordingly. Every oven is different, and the level of dough development and the size of the loaves will also affect the speed of baking. As a general rule, smaller loaves can be baked at a slightly warmer temperature and for a shorter period, while larger loaves require a slightly cooler temperature and longer baking time. An airy dough often bakes faster, while a heavy dough usually needs a bit more time to be thoroughly cooked inside. You can judge whether the bread is sufficiently baked by tapping it as you take it out of the oven. A bread that hasn't been cooked sufficiently sounds dull, a bread that is baked through sounds hollow.

If you notice the crust is browning too rapidly, it is better to turn down the temperature rather than reduce the baking time. Baking for too little time can cause the crumb to be less well-cooked, making it slightly sticky, and also the flavor will be less developed.

The times indicated for the primary fermentation and proofing, taken together with the dough temperature and the information regarding whether or not the dough is placed in the fridge, the amount of mixing or kneading, the autolyse, and the baking surface, all give you a lot of information on the qualities of the bread you will be making. With a bit of experience, and understanding the processes at work, you will be able to compare recipes very quickly and make adjustments when needed.

Recipes

You will find a lot of similarities in the processes, ingredients, and quantities within the recipes. But slight differences, such as a different way of shaping, a shorter or longer resting time, or varying amounts of water, can make for very different breads. As you master these recipes you will find yourself baking some of France's and Italy's tastiest classic breads in their best imaginable form.

I selected the recipes, which include the main types of French bread and some variants such as Italian pizza dough, *Stollen* (Dutch or German Christmas bread), *brioche*, and Jewish *challah*, because they cover a wide range of techniques, and will help you to understand the effect your choices will have on flavor, crust, structure, and keeping qualities. At the same time, I have provided alternative methods which will show you how you can obtain similar results while adjusting the process to suit your own schedule.

Baguette tradition

The first, most basic, recipe to try is also one of the finest and purest recipes. The baguette, and specifically the "*baguette tradition*". Tradition in this case stands for quite a small baguette, made with a relatively soft (moist) dough given plenty of time for development, kneaded very little, weighed by hand, and shaped rather loosely. The result is an open structured loaf with large alveoli, a slightly beige crumb with a very full, delicate, and pure flavor with hints of roasted nuts, alongside some sweetness and a nice crunchy crust. Making a *baguette tradition* is very much like developing the taste of the flour to its maximum, without adding sourdough. This type of baguette has become very popular recently in France, a sort of reinvention of tradition, and in its pure form it is probably the best baguette to be had. It's not exactly a protected label however, and it's rare to find it in its pure and artisanal form – in particular, "weighed and shaped by hand" and the extended development are not often taken literally in professional bakeries.

Two methods of making the dough are provided below. While both lead more or less to the same result, they give you the opportunity to work with two very different schedules. The first method involves a short primary fermentation, after which the dough undergoes a long proofing in the fridge. The second method is based on a long, extended primary fermentation at a low temperature, and a short proofing. If you prefer and have the time, long proofing in the fridge is also possible for the second method. There are some differences in results between the two methods: prolonged proofing slightly intensifies the flavor, regardless of the length of time of the primary fermentation. And shorter proofing makes it possible for the dough to hold its shape a bit better, resulting in a larger volume and a more pronounced *grigne*. But these differences are minor – it is also just a matter of your preferred schedule, when it suits you best to shape the loaves.

These quantities are
for four to six baguettes

Ingredients

bread flour 1000 grams
type T55 or T65, medium strength, extensible
water 630-680 grams (63-68%)
salt 20 grams (2%)
yeast 2 grams (0.2%)

autolyse 45 minutes
kneading no kneading, except for the mixing of ingredients
weight of a dough piece: about 250-400 grams, depending
on the size of your oven

Method 1: short primary fermentation, prolonged proofing

Dough temperature after mixing and autolyse: 75°F (24°C).

Resting time (primary fermentation): about three hours partly
at room temperature, partly in the fridge, with one fold half
way; at the end the dough should feel airy.

Pré-façonnage: rolls, followed by about 5 to 15 minutes resting.

Façonnage: shape into a baguette, taking special attention not to
push out any of the gases.

Resting time (proofing): overnight in the fridge (12 to
30 hours); the baguettes should be airy, but still have some
strength when touched. Pay attention: As the dough is cold it
will feel relatively firm.

Method 2: prolonged primary fermentation, short proofing

Dough temperature after mixing and autolyse: 54°F (12°C).

Resting time (primary fermentation): about 12-24 hours partly at room temperature or directly in the fridge, with folding once halfway, but at least three hours before shaping; at the end the dough should feel airy (but also relatively strong because of its low temperature).

Pré-façonnage: rolls, followed by about 15 minutes resting.

Façonnage: shape into a baguette, taking particular care not to push out any of the gases, but closing the seam well, especially if the proofing will be relatively short and at room temperature.

Resting time (proofing): about two to three hours at room temperature or again in the fridge (12 to 20 hours); the baguettes should be airy, but still have some strength when touched.

Baking

Baking in a professional stone oven: 480°F (250°C), with only moderate steam; open the valves after about 10 minutes, to ensure a dry environment for the second part of the baking.

Baking at home with a baking stone: preheat the oven and stone to the highest temperature possible; try to create ample steam. Bake at 440°F (230°C). Pay attention while baking and if necessary, adjust the temperature.

Scoring: score three incisions on the top of the bread just before baking.

Baking time: about 20-25 minutes or until the crust is well developed and nicely browned.

Baguette blanche

The *baguette blanche* is the classic French baguette, which can be bought in any supermarket. It has a very thin dry crust, and a very light, airy, consistent, white crumb. The flavor is not particularly pronounced and rather bland. It will be fresh for a maximum of four hours and is best eaten immediately after it has cooled down. Its main quality is its lightness. It is made with the same ingredients as the *baguette tradition* but is handled more roughly (whether made by hand or with a machine – in both cases the dough is thoroughly degassed during weighing and shaping) and undergoes an intensive kneading process and a much shorter development.

Generally, this bread requires about 0.67% instant yeast (or about 2% fresh yeast), autolyse is skipped and it is kneaded intensively using a professional dough machine until the flour loses color and reaches a temperature of about 82°F (28°C). The development time (especially the primary fermentation, i.e. before shaping) is shortened as much as possible. Following this process, you will be rewarded with very light and airy baguettes in no time.

Photo: baguette tradition on the left, baguette blanche on the right

Working at home, it is actually probably easier to end up with a slightly improved version of this standard baguette. Your kneading will not be as intensive and you could make use of the autolyse period. You could easily use a bit less yeast and extend the primary fermentation to two or three hours before shaping, and the proofing to half an hour. These improvements will mean you retain more flavor, though possibly compromising somewhat in whiteness and volume. The bread will also stay fresh a bit longer.

It is also possible to make *baguette blanche* with a starter dough. This classic variation is also included below.

These quantities are
for four to six baguettes

Ingredients

bread flour 1000 grams
type T55 or T65, medium strength, extensible
water 600-660 grams (60-66%)
salt 20 grams (2%)
yeast 2-8 grams (0.2-0.8%)

autolyse none, or 20 minutes
kneading intensive kneading
weight of a dough piece: about 250-400 grams, depending
on the size of your oven

Method

Dough temperature after mixing and autolyse: 75°F to 81°F
(24°C to 27°C).

Resting time (primary fermentation): about 30 minutes to
1.5 hours at room temperature at the end of which the dough
should feel airy and have about doubled in size.

Pré-façonnage: rolls, followed by about 10 to 15 minutes resting.

Façonnage: shape into a baguette, degassing the dough pieces
and paying special attention to closing the seams very precisely.

Resting time (proofing): 15 minutes to 1.5 hours; the baguettes
should be airy, but still have some strength when touched.

Baking

Baking in a professional stone oven: 480°F (250°C), with
moderate steam; open the valves after about 10 minutes, to
ensure a dry environment for the second part of the baking; or
use a rotary oven with baguette racks, to get an even lighter
crust.

Baking at home with a baking stone: preheat the oven and stone
to the highest temperature possible; try to create ample steam;
or bake on a tray. Bake at 430°F (220°C). Pay attention while
baking and, if necessary, adjust the temperature.

Scoring: score three incisions on the top of the bread just before baking.

Baking time: about 20-25 minutes or until the crust is well developed and is lightly browned.

With a starter

A compromise between the two methods for making baguette could be the use of a starter (whether *pâte fermentée* or poolish), thus adding flavor and acidity while otherwise following the procedure as described above (preferably the slightly improved version, carried out by hand). The bread will be much less dry and stay fresh for longer, and taste far less bland. This type of baguette has long been the standard of the improved, artisan baguette, before the reinvention of the *baguette tradition*.

To proceed, replace some of the flour, water, and yeast in the original recipe with the poolish. Ideally you would make the poolish the day before and then leave it to develop slowly in the fridge. It is also possible to make the poolish just a few hours before starting the dough, using water at a temperature of about 75°F (24°C) and allowing the dough to develop at room temperature for about two hours. Flavor development will be slightly less pronounced, and there will be less acidity but it will still considerably improve the quality of the baguettes you will be making. Add the poolish to the dough, preferably after autolyse and before the primary fermentation. If the dough is not liquid enough to be mixed well without the poolish, you can add the poolish before the autolyse to facilitate mixing.

For example:

Poolish	Dough
flour 400 grams (40%)	**flour** 600 grams (60%)
water 320 grams (32%)	**water** 280-320 grams (28%-32%)
yeast 2 grams (0.2%)	**salt** 20 grams (2%)
	yeast none or 4 grams (0-0.4%)

Cutting baguette à l'ancienne

Baguette à l'ancienne coming out of the oven

Baguette
à l'ancienne

I would like to express my gratitude to Gosselin bakery and to Peter Reinhart, in whose book I first encountered this method

These quantities are
for four to six baguettes

This method is very much like the *baguette tradition*, except that it takes it one step further. Rather than shaping loosely, the process of shaping is skipped completely. You can also add more water to the dough. These modifications result in a loss of the *grigne* and the crusty bite of the *baguette tradition*, but in return, you will get an even more open structure, and an even more pronounced flavor. This recipe can also be baked as a type of *ciabatta* (a "slipper" in Italian, a large, soft and airy but rather flat bread). Using cold water jumpstarts the process of amylase turning starch into sugars, and because you do not shape the dough, hardly any degassing occurs. Once you get used to handling this moist dough, the process is very simple and straightforward and involves very little effort.

Ingredients

bread flour 1000 grams
type T55 or T65, medium strength, extensible
water 720-800 grams (72-80%)
salt 20 grams (2%)
yeast 2 grams (0.2%)

autolyse 45 minutes
kneading no kneading, except for the mixing of ingredients
weight of a dough piece as you cut it, there is no weighing involved; you can choose the size and shape

Method

Dough temperature after mixing and autolyse: 46°F to 50°F (8°C to 10°C); use literally ice-cold water and, during autolyse, put the dough back in the fridge. The easiest way to mix it is to use a hand mixer with dough hooks.

Resting time: overnight in the fridge (12 to 30 hours); the dough should be very airy and light, but still have some strength when touched, and hold its shape. To reinforce the dough, fold between one and three times depending on the level of hydration. If you feel the dough is not rising fast enough, take it out of the fridge three to six hours before baking.

Baking

To remove the dough from the container in which it has been developing, turn the box or bowl upside down over a very well-floured surface. With some prodding the dough will drop onto the surface. Sprinkle flour on the top of the dough too and use a dough cutter to cut out either small buns or baguettes. Transfer them carefully but quickly onto a dough peel lined with baking parchment and dusted with semolina flour.

Baking in a professional stone oven: 480°F (250°C), with moderate steam; open the valves after about 10 minutes, to ensure a dry environment for the second part of the baking.

Baking at home on a baking stone: preheat the oven and stone to the highest temperature possible; try to create ample steam. Bake at 440°F (230°C). Pay attention while baking and if necessary, adjust the temperature.

Scoring: if the dough is relatively firm, score three incisions on the top of the bread just before baking

Baking time: about 20-25 minutes or until the crust is well developed and has a beautiful color.

Pavé

Pavé is a bread with an almost rectangular shape, *pavé* being the name of a street tile – the ones over which cyclists struggle to make it from Paris to Roubaix in one of the most famous annual bike races. It can be made with dough similar to that of a baguette, the *baguette tradition* dough giving the best results. Important to a successful *pavé* is to allow for a proper (quite high) level of development during the primary fermentation. The bread should then be shaped rather quickly, maintaining good surface tension. Make a seam but do not seal it firmly, so that it can open up during baking. To allow this to happen, the bread should be placed "upside down" for baking, with the seam on top. The *pavé* differs from the baguette in its proportion of crust to crumb, its size, and to some extent in its flavor. The bigger dough piece from which a *pavé* is made will cool down more slowly than a baguette when given a cold second resting period and requires a longer baking time. The dough is also handled differently than a baguette during shaping. The result is a different proportion of crust and crumb, and a different flavor from a baguette, even though the *pavé* is made from exactly the same dough. Try it: Make the two kinds of bread the same day from the same dough.

These quantities are for three *pavés*

Ingredients

bread flour 1000 grams
type T55 or T65, medium strength, extensible
water 600-660 grams of water (60-66%)
salt 20 grams (2%)
yeast 2 grams (0.2%)

autolyse 45 minutes
kneading no kneading, except for the mixing of ingredients
weight of a dough piece about 500 grams

Method

As with the *baguette tradition*, see pages 118-121. You can use both methods described there, with either a short primary fermentation or a short proofing. But ensure that the dough has risen sufficiently before shaping, and that the resting period after shaping is not too long (maximum of 15-18 hours in the

fridge). The dough piece should still have enough tension to open up by itself, and the seam should still be visible.

Shaping

To shape a *pavé*, first pre-shape into rolls, just like you would for a baguette (see page 76). To obtain the final shape, follow these steps:

Place a roll in front of you, with the seam up and turned 90 degrees.
Fold the far edge towards you, about two thirds of the way over the dough.
Then fold the edge closest to you over the dough, again about two thirds of the way.
Again, take the edge close to you and fold over the dough, as if you were tucking it in, leaving the seam in the center without closing it.
Keep your fingers on the seam, so you can feel where it is, and place the bread on a *couche* with the seam down and exactly in the center.

Three things are especially important:
- Work very quickly, so that the dough can go back in the fridge before it gets too warm. The proofing should not be too long, as the pieces will need to have a strong oven spring to burst open on their own, without incision.

- Make a clear, straight seam, right in the middle, but don't close it.

- Maintain surface tension on the dough. To achieve this, repeat the tucking-in motion towards the end once or twice more, if necessary, but avoid tearing the dough. Make sure the tension is the same everywhere.

Baking

Upside down, with no incision, for about 35 to 40 minutes, with a decreasing temperature, as for a *baguette tradition*. Make sure that the loaves do not color too quickly, so they can have the full baking time and are thoroughly cooked inside.

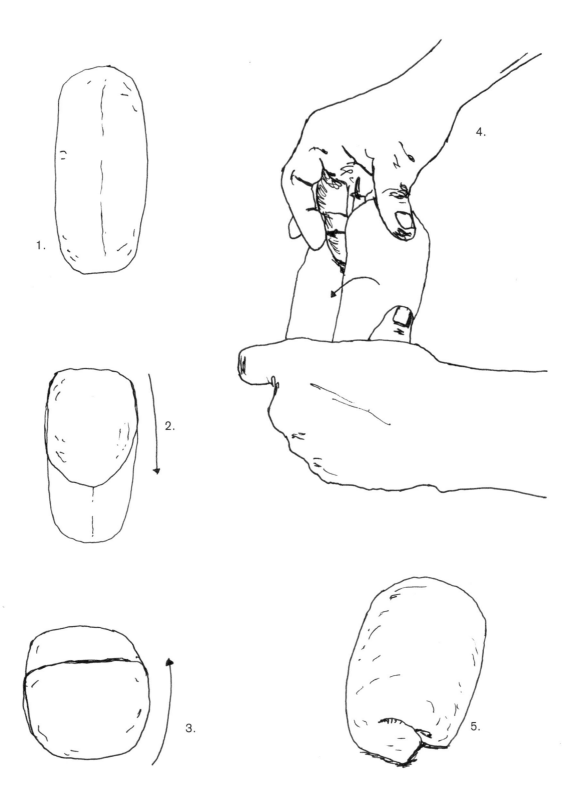

Petit pain with walnut and fig, white petit pain

Petits pains

Any of the baguette recipes provided above can be used to make *petits pains*, small bread rolls. There are different ways to proceed.

To make small, round *petits pains*, cut small pieces of the dough when weighing, anything between 40 and 80 grams. Pre-shape them into small balls, which can be formed within the palm of your hand, making round movements as you would for a bigger *boule* (see page 77) and using the work surface to create tension. Shape by repeating the same movement, after having left the dough pieces to rest for several minutes. Before baking, you can score a straight line, a cross, or a rectangle using a *lame* (a razor or very sharp knife, see page 233), depending on your preference.

To make *pistolets* (baguette buns), cut slightly bigger pieces, up to 150 grams. Pre-shape into balls, and then make the final shape as for a *batard* (page 81) after having let the dough pieces rest for 10 to 15 minutes. Before baking, score the loaf with a straight line.

An alternative method is to follow the recipe for making regular baguettes as usual and cut the loaves into *petits pains* or *pistolets* immediately before they go into the oven. To do so, first score the baguettes with a straight incision using the *lame*. Then, using sharp scissors held at 45 degrees to the work surface, lift the baguette slightly where you want to cut it, slide the scissors underneath, and make the cut, repeating until the loaf is divided into multiple small rolls. The shape will be slightly rougher and more irregular, but very nice. Bakeries working on a larger scale use this method as a very quick way to make hundreds of small rolls.

Photo: we also make petits pains with wholemeal, grey, and walnut and fig doughs in our bakery

Épi

An *épi* is another shape of loaf that can be made with any baguette dough. The name "*épi*" is French for an ear of wheat, the shape that the bread resembles. It is made by making a series of cuts with sharp scissors into a baguette at regular intervals. The cuts should be made just before the bread is put into the oven and after having made a straight incision with a *lame*. Hold the scissors at an angle of 45 degrees, without lifting the dough, and make sure that you do not cut all the way through the baguette, so that the baguette splits in places but remains a single loaf. After each cut, immediately twist the section to one side of the center of the loaf, alternating to the left and to the right each time. *Épi* is a very beautiful bread, very nice to have either for breakfast or to accompany dinner.

Sourdough

Of course, there is no single recipe for sourdough bread, as there are many different kinds of bread that can be made with sourdough. Here, I will single out two of the most common found in France as well as in North America: a sourdough *boule*, using a grey type 80 flour (*bise*), and a sourdough *batard* using a white, type 65, flour. Both are traditional country breads and are very similar to breads found in traditional villages in Italy, Portugal, Switzerland, or Germany – though, depending on the region and country, with a different emphasis on lightness or density, acidity, crust, and so on. We will make the *boule* with a stronger, denser, and more acidic sourdough, and the *batard* with a lighter, liquid sourdough. This provides an example of both methods and of the differences in texture and flavor they achieve. The *boule* will be slightly denser, and have a more pronounced acidic flavor, while the *batard* will have a very open, airy structure and a full, rich, but not acidic flavor. Both will have strong, flavorful crusts and will keep well for several days.

In our bakery, we make both of these breads with liquid sourdough. The recipes for all of these variations are identical, except for the quantity of water added to compensate for the amount of hydration in the sourdough itself.

When using liquid sourdough, the sourdough can be mixed with the dough before autolyse. The dough will otherwise not be hydrated enough to be mixed properly, because a larger proportion of the water in the dough comes from the sourdough itself. When using firm sourdough it should be added to the dough after autolyse.

I will describe one basic method – which can certainly be varied successfully, e.g. by making the proofing shorter at room temperature, rather than the prolonged proofing in the fridge. This will make the acidic flavors less pronounced, but at the same time the amylase working on the starches will produce fewer sugars. Thus, the bread will literally have a less fully developed flavor but will be ideal if you are looking for low acidity and a lighter crust.

Sourdough boule

These quantities are
for one boule

Ingredients

bread flour 400 grams
type T80, medium strength
sourdough 200 grams (proportion flour to water: 2:1)
water 265-300 grams
(with the water in the sourdough 62-69%)
salt 10 grams (2%)

autolyse 45 minutes (flour and water)
kneading no kneading, except for the mixing of ingredients
weight of a dough piece about 875-900 grams

Method

Dough temperature after mixing and autolyse: 79°F (26°C).

Resting time (primary fermentation): about 2-3 hours at room temperature with one fold halfway; at the end the dough should feel airy.

Pré-façonnage: balls, followed by about 15 minutes resting.

Façonnage: shape into a *boule* using the technique demonstrated in the drawings, taking care to maintain adequate tension but not closing the seam too tightly.

Resting time (proofing): overnight in the fridge (12 to 16 hours); the *boule* should be airy, but still have some strength when touched. Please note: As the dough is cold it will feel relatively firm.

Baking

Baking in a professional stone oven: 480°F (250°C), with moderate steam; open the valves after about 30 minutes, to ensure a dry environment for the last part of the baking. After the first 15 minutes, slowly let the temperature fall to 440°F (230°C).

Baking at home with a baking stone: preheat the oven and stone to the highest temperature possible; try to create ample steam; slowly let the temperature fall after the bread has opened up and started to develop its initial, light coloring. Don't let the bread brown too quickly; adjust the temperature to ensure you can give it the full baking time.

Scoring: do not score the loaf, but bake the bread upside down, to let it open up by itself along the seams created by shaping; alternatively, score four incisions on the top of the bread just before baking (see illustration).

Baking time: about 45-55 minutes or until the crust is well developed and has a good color, and the bread is baked through.

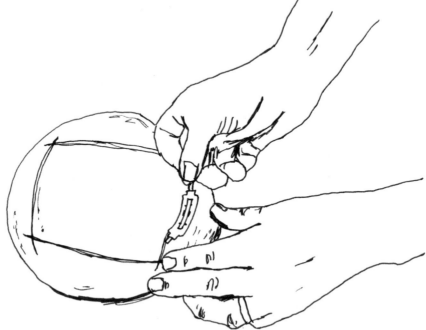

Sourdough boules

Sourdough batard

Sourdough batard

These quantities are
for two batards

Ingredients

bread flour 640 grams
type T65, medium strength
sourdough 320 grams (proportion flour to water: 1:1)
water 335-375 grams
(with the water in the sourdough 62-67%)
salt 16 grams (2%)

autolyse 45 minutes (flour, water and sourdough)
kneading no kneading, except for the mixing of ingredients
weight of a dough piece about 650 grams

Method

Dough temperature after mixing and autolyse: 79°F (26°C).

Resting time (primary fermentation): about 2-3 hours at room temperature with one fold halfway; at the end the dough should feel airy.

Pré-façonnage: balls, followed by about 15 minutes resting.

Façonnage: shape into a *batard*, taking special care to maintain adequate tension and to close the seam firmly.

Resting time (proofing): overnight in the fridge (12 to 18 hours); the *batards* should be airy, but still have some strength when touched. Please note: As the dough is cold it will feel relatively firm.

Baking

Baking in a professional stone oven: 480°F (250°C), with moderate steam; open the valves after about 30 minutes, to ensure a dry environment for the last part of the baking. After the first 15 minutes, slowly let the temperature fall to 440°F (230°C).

Baking at home with a baking stone: preheat the oven and stone to the highest temperature possible, try to create ample steam; slowly let the temperature fall after the bread has opened up and started to develop its first, light coloring. Make sure the breads don't color too quickly so that you can give them the full baking time.

Scoring: score one incision on the top of the bread just before baking.

Baking time: about 40-45 minutes or until the crust is well developed and has a good color, and the bread is baked through.

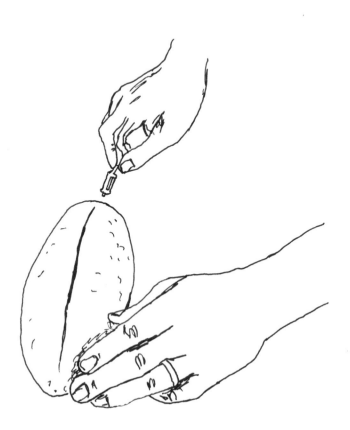

Wholemeal

Wholemeal flour is characterized by its high fiber content, impacting on flavor as well as on baking qualities. Choosing wholemeal flour is not just a case of replacing one type of flour with another.

The main characteristic of wholemeal flour, from a baker's point of view, is that it will produce a denser loaf, with smaller alveoli. The fiber present in wholemeal flour absorbs more water than white flour and leaves a less hydrated dough. When insufficiently hydrated, enzymes, yeast, and bacteria will all work or reproduce more slowly. The bread will then tend to stay even more dense.

The density and slow development of the dough may induce you to give it a longer fermentation time but this will result in an acidic flavor. Even if this is avoided, the density of the dough will favor anaerobic bacteria which produce acetic acids, also raising the acidic flavor profile of the loaf. The best way to compensate for the effects of wholemeal flour on dough development is simply to increase the level of hydration.

Below we give two recipes as a starting point for working with wholemeal flour, one a sourdough *boule* using a liquid sourdough, the other also a *boule*, but using yeast. You will find that the sourdough *boule* recipe is exactly the same as the recipe for a sourdough *batard*, except that the level of hydration is increased and the temperature during the second half of baking is slightly lower, to enable the denser bread to bake well on the inside. The recipe with yeast is very similar to that of a baguette. This similarity will actually help you to understand the basic workings of bread recipes in general. In the end it comes down to very simple procedures that are applicable to many different varieties of breads, carried out with attention to those few details which do change, and most importantly, with a "feel" for the process and its dynamics.

Photo: wholemeal boule on a couche

Wholemeal
sourdough boule

These quantities are
for one boule

Ingredients

bread flour 400 grams
type T150, medium strength
sourdough 200 grams (proportion of flour to water: 1:1)
water 220-250 grams
(together with the water in the sourdough 64-70%)
salt 10 grams (2%)

autolyse 45 minutes (flour, water, and sourdough)
kneading no kneading, except for the mixing of ingredients
weight of a dough piece about 875 grams

Method

Dough temperature after mixing and autolyse: 79°F (26°C).

Resting time (primary fermentation): about 2-3 hours at room temperature with one fold halfway; at the end the dough should feel airy.

Pré-façonnage: balls, followed by about 15 minutes resting.

Façonnage: shape into a *boule* using the technique demonstrated in the drawings, paying special attention to maintaining adequate tension but not closing the seam too tightly.

Resting time (proofing): overnight in the fridge (12 to 18 hours); the *boule* should be airy, but still have some strength when touched. Please note: As the dough is cold it will feel relatively firm.

Baking

Baking in a professional stone oven: 480°F (250°C), with moderate steam; open the valves after about 30 minutes, to ensure a dry environment for the last part of the baking. After the first 15 minutes, slowly let the temperature fall to 430°F (220°C).

Baking at home with a baking stone: preheat the oven and stone to the highest temperature possible, try to create ample steam; slowly let the temperature fall after the bread has opened up and started to develop its first, light coloring.

Scoring: bake the bread upside down, to let it open up by itself along the seams created by shaping, or alternatively score four incisions on the top of the bread just before baking (see the illustration on page 143).

Baking time: about 40-50 minutes or until the crust is well-developed and has a good color, and the bread is baked through.

Take extra care with wholemeal bread that the baking temperature is not too high. As the dough is slightly more compact it also bakes a bit more slowly on the inside. Be sure to give the bread the full baking time.

Wholemeal
yeast boule

These quantities are
for one boule

Ingredients

bread flour 500 grams
type T150, medium strength
water 320-350 grams (64 to 74%)
salt 10 grams (2%)
yeast 1 gram (0.2%)

autolyse 45 minutes
kneading no kneading, except for the mixing of ingredients
weight of a dough piece about 850 grams

Method

Dough temperature after mixing and autolyse: 75°F (24°C).

Resting time (primary fermentation): about 2-3 hours at room temperature, with one fold halfway; at the end the dough should feel airy, but might not have doubled in size.

Pré-façonnage: balls, followed by about 15 minutes resting.

Façonnage: shape into a *boule* using the technique demonstrated in the drawings, taking special care that adequate tension is maintained but do not close the seam too tightly.

Resting time (proofing): overnight in the fridge (12 to 30 hours); the *boule* should be airy, but still have some strength when touched. Please note: As the dough is cold it will feel relatively firm.

Baking

Baking in a professional stone oven: 480°F (250°C), with moderate steam; open the valves after about 30 minutes, to ensure a dry environment for the last part of the baking. After the first 15 minutes, slowly let the temperature fall to 430°F (220°C).

Baking at home with a baking stone: preheat the oven and stone to the highest temperature possible, try to create ample steam; slowly let the temperature fall after the bread has opened up and started to develop its first, light coloring.

Scoring: bake the bread upside down, to let it open up by itself on the seams created by shaping, or score four incisions on the top of the bread just before baking (see the illustration on page 143).

Baking time: about 40-50 minutes or until the crust is well developed and has a good color, and the bread is baked through.

Take extra care with wholemeal bread that the baking temperature is not too high. As the dough is slightly more compact it also bakes a bit more slowly on the inside. Be sure to give the bread the full baking time.

Rye bread

Of course, it is possible to replace the wheat flour commonly used for bread baking with flour made from all sorts of different grains. As a general rule, remember that wheat flour is used for its specific capacity to form gluten, the strings of protein that retain gases, and that replacing it may lead to very dense breads. Thus, often, the best choice may be to replace only a portion of the wheat flour.

Here we choose to replace two-thirds of the wheat flour in a dough with rye flour. In France, this proportion is required to be able to label a loaf as rye bread (*pain de seigle*). If less than 65% rye flour is used, the bread has to be called "bread with rye" (*pain au seigle*).

Breads made with only rye flour, such as a traditional Dutch rye bread, are certainly worthwhile to bake but are completely different and made according to different principles outside of the scope of this book.

When working with rye flour (in a mixed rye and wheat flour bread) take note of the following:

- Rye flour has fewer proteins than wheat flour, but more importantly, the pentosans in rye flour (a particular kind of fiber often referred to as "flour gum") actually absorb such a large quantity of water, to the extent that their inflation gets in the way of gluten formation. That is, the pentosans make it more difficult for the proteins to "find each other" and form strings.

- Rye flour absorbs and retains more water than wheat flour. Always ensure the dough is sufficiently hydrated, to avoid the bread from becoming too dry and to make sure enzymatic processes and fermentation are not slowed down too much. Rye dough will and should feel relatively sticky.

- As fewer gluten strands are formed, rye flour itself will not be able to retain gases, and the loaf will be denser, requiring slower, more thorough baking.

- The crust will become soft relatively quickly, as the water content in the bread will be relatively high; this is another reason to ensure a sufficient baking time.

- Mixing should not be too intense. The relatively small amount of gluten will easily overdevelop and result in a weaker dough and denser loaf.

- Enzymes in rye flour remain active for a longer time while baking than those found in wheat flour, breaking down starches and leading to a mushy, sticky crumb. The use of sourdough, or the addition of acidity by using vinegar, slows down enzymatic activity, counterbalancing this tendency. Kept in check, the prolonged activity of enzymes actually makes for a more tender crumb, which stays fresh longer.

- The increased acidity in the dough by using sourdough also benefits the capacity of the rye flour to form gluten networks.

- Rye bread needs a longer time to settle and is often at its best half a day or a full day after baking; the pentosans retain moisture very well even after baking.

Ingredients

bread flour 135 grams
type T65, medium strength
rye flour 585 grams
type 130, medium strength
sourdough 360 grams (proportion flour to water: 1:1)
water 400-450 grams (together with the water in the sourdough 65-70%)
salt 18 grams (2%)

These quantities are for three rye loaves

autolyse 45 minutes (flour, water, and sourdough)
kneading no kneading, except for the mixing of ingredients
weight of a dough piece about 500 grams

Method

Dough temperature after mixing and autolyse: 79°F (26°C).

Resting time (primary fermentation): about 2-3 hours at room temperature with one fold halfway; at the end the dough should feel airy.

Pré-façonnage: balls, followed by about 15 minutes resting.
Façonnage: shape into a *batard*, taking special care that
adequate tension is maintained and the seam is firmly closed.

Resting time (proofing): overnight in the fridge (12 to 18
hours); the *batards* should be airy, but still have some strength
when touched. Please note: As the dough is cold it will feel
relatively firm.

Baking

Baking in a professional stone oven: 480°F (250°C), with
moderate steam; open the valves after about 30 minutes, to
ensure a dry environment for the last part of the baking. After
the first 15 minutes, slowly let the temperature fall to 440°F
(230°C).

Baking at home with a baking stone: preheat the oven and
stone to the highest temperature possible, try to create ample
steam; slowly let the temperature fall after the bread has
opened up and started to develop its first, light coloring. Don't
let the breads color too quickly; ensure you can give them the
full baking time.

Scoring: lighty dust with rye flour, using a sieve. Cut a *coupe
polka* using a sharp knife just before baking (see illustration on
page 161).

Baking time: about 40-50 minutes or until the crust is well
developed and has a good color, and the bread is baked
through.

Pain au noix

figs, blue cheese

I very much like the taste of walnuts in bread. It's one of the classic combinations which really works. The walnuts give a bit of walnut oil to the dough, which adds a unique flavor to the bread as a whole and slightly changes its color, especially if you roast the walnuts and break them partially just before adding them to the dough. Adding the walnuts after autolyse and initial kneading means the oil (fat, that is) is only added to the dough after the gluten networks have already started to form, making it possible for the bread to maintain the open structure typical of French bread. Fats encapsulate the gluten, so had you added the walnuts earlier in the process, the gluten strings would have remained smaller, and the alveoli finer.

Adding dried figs to a dough also changes its nature. The figs will give off sugar while being mixed in, causing the crust to bake faster and become darker, and absorb more water, making the loaf slightly denser and heavier. Meanwhile the figs themselves remain slightly moist and sweet, contrasting with the heavy, dark crust and denser crumb. Figs can be added to the dough by themselves, but also in combination with walnuts.

Cheeses change their flavor while being baked, and I prefer by far to have good bread with good cheese, rather than add the cheese to the dough. One exception is the use of a strong and salty blue cheese incorporated into the dough. A high quality roquefort would just melt into the dough and lose all the subtleties of its flavor. But small pieces of a lesser quality Danish Blue can, if mixed in very carefully, retain their shape, creating a contrast within the bread, and losing their sharpness while baking. Like with figs, adding both walnuts and blue cheese to a dough actually makes a nicely balanced combination.

To make any of these breads, sourdough is the most suitable basis. It provides a sturdy base, balancing the flavor of the walnuts, figs, or cheese. Included here for reference are the recipes we use in our bakery – that is, one recipe for walnut bread or walnut and fig bread, and one recipe for a walnut and blue cheese bread. The walnut and walnut and fig bread are shaped into *batards*, while the walnut and blue cheese bread is shaped into a small *boule* or *miche*. The first recipe is very

Walnut and walnut and fig breads in the bakery shop

much like any sourdough bread. The recipe with blue cheese does need some adjustments. To compensate for the saltiness of the cheese, we add less salt to the dough. And to make sure the cheese doesn't mix into the dough completely, we use an alternative technique for adding the cheese and for shaping the loaf.

Walnut /
Walnut and fig

To make walnut bread, all that is needed is to leave out the figs in this recipe; everything else stays the same

These quantities are for two walnut / walnut and fig loaves

Ingredients

bread flour 480 grams
type T80, medium strength
sourdough 240 grams (proportion flour to water: 1:1)
water 275-290 grams (65-68%)
salt 12 grams (2%)
dried figs 190 grams, cut into quarters (32%)
walnuts 125 grams, lightly roasted and then cooled down (21%)

autolyse 45 minutes (flour, water, and sourdough)
kneading no kneading, except for the mixing of ingredients
weight of a dough piece about 650 grams

Method

Dough temperature after mixing and autolyse: 79°F (26°C); add the walnuts and figs after autolyse, towards the end of mixing, so that they don't break the internal structure of the dough too much; break a few of the walnuts just before adding them, so that some of the oil from the walnuts mixes into the dough.

Resting time (primary fermentation): about 2-3 hours at room temperature with one fold halfway; at the end the dough should feel airy.

Pré-façonnage: balls, followed by about 15 minutes resting.

Façonnage: shape into a *batard*, taking special care to maintain adequate tension and to close the seam tightly.

Resting time (proofing): overnight in the fridge (12 to 18 hours); the bread should be airy, but still have some strength when touched. Please note: As the dough is cold it will feel relatively firm. Moreover, if you touch the dough at a spot where there is a walnut or a piece of fig directly underneath the surface, it will feel a bit stronger; judge how the dough feels where there are no nuts or figs.

Baking

Baking in a professional stone oven: 480°F (250°C), with moderate steam; open the valves after about 30 minutes, to ensure a dry environment for the last part of the baking. After the first 15 minutes, slowly let the temperature fall to 435°F (225°C).

Baking at home with a baking stone: preheat the oven and stone to the highest temperature possible, try to create ample steam; slowly let the temperature fall after the bread has opened up and started to develop its first, light coloring. Don't let the breads color too quickly; ensure you can give them the full baking time.

Scoring: cut a *coupe polka* using a sharp knife just before baking.

Baking time: bake about 35-40 minutes or until the crust is well developed and has a good color, dark, because of the sugar from the figs, but not burned, and the bread is baked through.

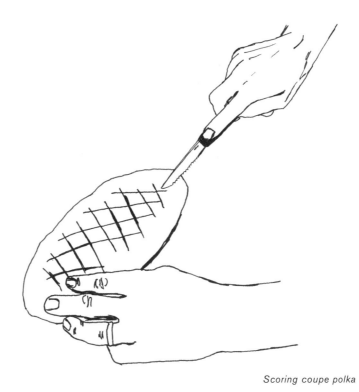

Scoring coupe polka

Walnut and fig and walnut

Walnut and blue cheese

Walnut and blue cheese

These quantities are for four walnut and blue cheese rolls

Ingredients

bread flour 400 grams
type T65, medium strength
sourdough 200 grams (proportion flour to water: 1:1)
water 220-240 grams (64-68%)
salt 7 grams (1.4%)
blue cheese 140 grams, strong and firm, such as Danish Blue, cut into small pieces and then placed back in the fridge (28%)
walnuts 125 grams, lightly roasted and then cooled down (25%)

autolyse 45 minutes (flour, water, and sourdough)
kneading no kneading, except for the mixing of ingredients
weight of a dough piece about 250 grams

Method

Dough temperature after mixing and autolyse: 79°F (26°C); add the walnuts after autolyse, after having briefly mixed in the salt; break a few of the walnuts just before adding them, so that some of the oil from the walnuts mixes into the dough. Mix in again briefly, but not perfectly, as the walnuts will be more evenly mixed into the dough while adding the blue cheese.

To add the blue cheese, flatten and stretch the dough on a slightly moist work surface. Scatter half of the cheese on the surface of the dough, making sure there is a bit of distance between the pieces so that they will remain individual chunks rather than one layer. Roll up the dough, turn it 90 degrees, horizontally, and flatten again, if necessary dampen the work surface to prevent sticking. Scatter the remaining cheese onto the dough and roll up again. Fold once and place it in a lightly floured or oiled container.

Resting time (primary fermentation): about 2-3 hours at room temperature with one fold halfway; at the end the dough should feel airy.

Façonnage: skipping *pré-façonnage*, shape carefully into balls using your hands, avoiding pushing the cheese into the dough

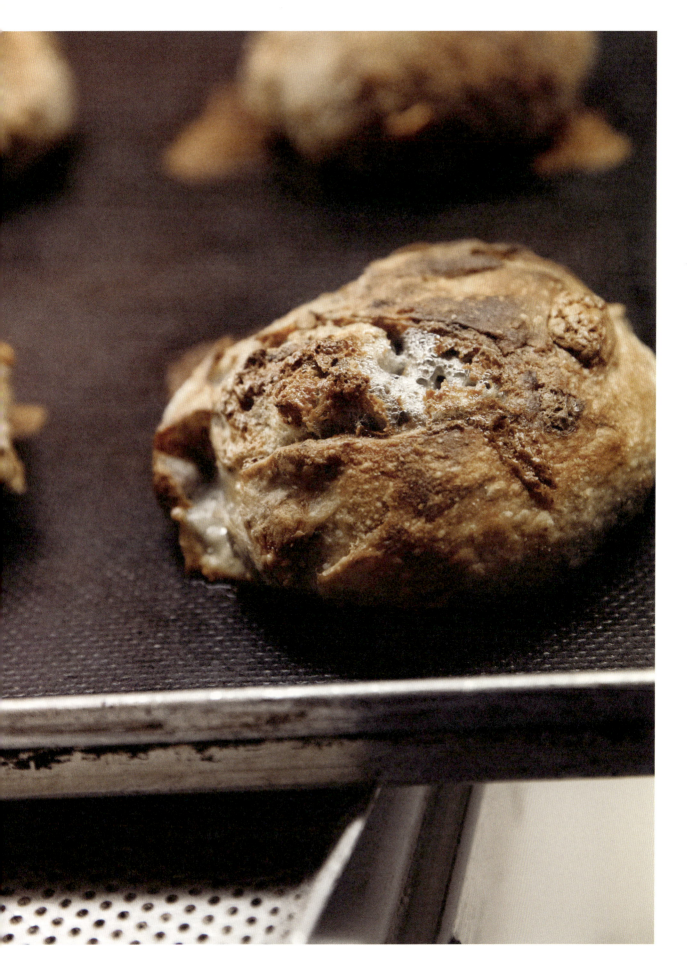

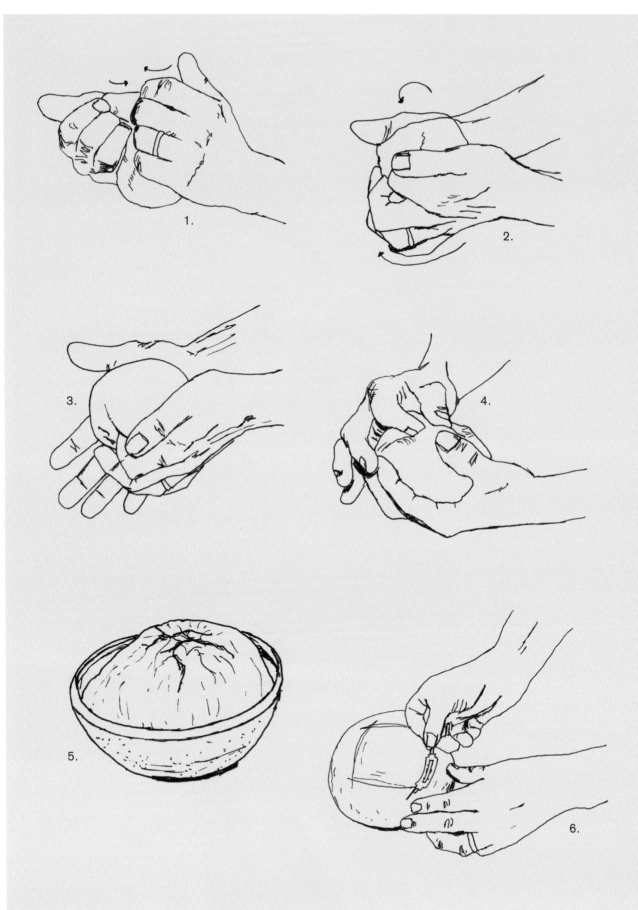

1.

2.

3.

4.

5.

6.

too much by folding the dough inwards again and again, changing your angle every time, until you have reached adequate tension; then close the seam firmly and place each ball into small round containers (e.g. small bowls) with the seam on top. The bowls should be lightly oiled (preferably with spray oil) and roughly sprinkled with semolina, to create a beautifully colorful crust on top of the bread after baking.

Resting time (proofing): overnight in the fridge (12 to 20 hours); the bread should be airy, but still have some strength when touched. Please note: As the dough is cold it will feel relatively firm.

Baking

Baking in a professional stone oven: 480°F (250°C) on top, 435°F (225°C) at the bottom, with moderate steam; open the valves after about 20 minutes, to ensure a dry environment for the last part of the baking.

Baking at home with a baking stone: preheat the oven and stone to the highest temperature possible, try to create ample steam; let the temperature fall after the bread has opened up and started to develop its first, light coloring.

To protect the stone floor from the melting cheese use baking paper and a dough peel to bake on the baking stone when baking at home, but when using a professional bakery oven, use a baking tray. Take the bread out of the bowls by holding them upside down just above the baking tray. This turns the bread over so that the seams are now on the bottom.

Make sure the bread doesn't color too quickly, so you can give the loaves the full baking time

Scoring: use a *lame* to score four lines in the shape of a # on the upper part of the bread just before baking.

Baking time: bake about 30 minutes or until the crust is well developed and has a good color, and the bread is baked through.

Pizza bianca

Pizza bianca is a specialty that comes from Rome. It is basically a pizza without topping. It is slightly thicker, and it rises a bit more while baking, becoming a flat kind of bread. Due to its exceptionally high water content the bread has a very open crumb with large alveoli, staying moist and fresh for a long time as well as having a fully developed flavor. Its crust is covered with olive oil and sea salt.

Pizza bianca can also be found in other parts of Italy and is sometimes known as a type of focaccia or *pizza pane*. Here we stick to the Roman version – and a Roman would not call it focaccia for sure. A focaccia has a soft, almost cake-like crumb, while the *pizza bianca* is chewy, with a strong, well-developed dough structure. The bread is up to two meters long and 80 centimeters wide, depending on the oven, and then cut into rectangular pieces which are sold individually. The pieces closer to the outside of the pizza are darker and crunchier, while the pieces on the inside are relatively lightly baked and soft.

To absorb the high amount of water needed, while maintaining a workable and well-developed dough, the *pizza bianca* dough is not mixed at once but given a series of turns in the dough mixer, and is folded later on in the process, to give it sufficient strength. It's one of the most challenging doughs to work on, but once mastered, also one of the most rewarding. Initially extremely sticky and almost impossible to fold, the dough eventually acquires a very silky texture, which is pleasant to the touch.

How much dough you will need to make for the *pizza bianca* depends on the size of the oven you use, how thick you want the bread to be, and if you are planning to bake it in one or two batches. This quantity is appropriate for a regular sized home oven, but if you would like the pizza to be a little thinner you can divide it into two pieces.

Ingredients

pizza flour 450 grams (90%)
type T45 or T55; in the Italian coding: "00" or "0"
finely ground durum wheat semolina (*semola di grano duro rimacinata*) 50 grams (10%)
water 425-450 grams (85-90%)
salt 10 grams (2%)
yeast 1.5 gram (0.3%)
olive oil extra *vergine* (for the topping)
sea salt not too fine, not too coarse (for the topping)

autolyse 45 minutes
kneading a few minutes of kneading before and after **autolyse**; then a series of turns
weight of a dough piece as the *pizza bianca* is cut after baking, there is no weighing involved (unless you want to divide the dough into several batches if it would otherwise be too big for your oven)

Method

Dough temperature after mixing and autolyse: 59°F to 64°F (15°C to 18°C). To mix, it is easiest to use a hand mixer with dough hooks. After autolyse, having mixed in the salt and yeast, let the dough rest for 15 minutes, then give it a very short turn if using a planetary mixer, or stir and pull for just a few seconds using a large spoon, for instance, while avoiding overworking. Repeat this three more times (so four in total), then let the dough rest for half an hour, and give it a final turn (or stir and pull). Put the dough in a well-oiled container and leave it to develop further in the fridge. After three to ten hours, fold the dough on a well-floured surface, using very quick movements (the dough will still be extremely sticky at this point) and put it back in the fridge again. If the dough has not yet acquired sufficient coherence and strength by this time, you can repeat this step once more after a few hours.

Resting time: overnight in the fridge (totaling 20 to 30 hours); the dough should be very airy and light, almost bubbly, very well developed, but still strong. To reinforce the dough, give the dough a turn one last time a few hours before baking. If you feel the dough has not developed enough, you could take it out of the fridge three to six hours before baking.

If your oven is too small, you can also divide the dough into two portions before the last fold and bake them one at a time.

Baking

Turn the dough directly onto a very well-floured peel (in our bakery we use both flour and rough semolina to prevent the dough from sticking). It is also possible to place baking paper on the peel (also dusted with semolina) to make it easier to slide the *pizza bianca* into the oven, along with the paper. Sprinkle flour over the dough, and extend it carefully, after flouring your hands. Lift it slightly when pulling it, creating a rectangle with a thickness of slightly more than half a centimeter. If the dough is springy, you can also extend it step by step, letting it rest for a few moments in between. Brush lightly with olive oil and sprinkle with sea salt. If the dough is too firm and not quite fully developed yet, you can also leave it on the peel for a few minutes or even a quarter of an hour. It will relax a little and quickly become more active but take care that it doesn't start to become sticky.

Baking in a professional stone oven: 480°F (250°C), with moderate steam; open the valves after about 15 minutes, to ensure a dry environment for the second part of the baking.

Baking at home with a baking stone: preheat the oven and stone to the highest temperature possible, try to create ample steam. Bake at 440°F (230°C). Pay attention while baking and if necessary, adjust the temperature.

Scoring: do not score the dough.

Baking time: about 25 to 30 minutes or until the crust is well developed and has a good color.

Shaping a pizza

Pizza

Pizza napoletana, in its simplicity, can be of a very high quality. A good traditional Italian pizza dough is made according to the same principles as a good bread dough, having undergone an extended proofing of 24 to 36 hours. Kneading is hardly necessary (though traditionally the dough usually is well kneaded). Folding the dough two or three times will give a far better result. To achieve sufficient extensibility the dough should be relatively moist, with a hydration level of around 65-70% allowing you to pre-shape it into balls and then later, after a sufficient rest, roll out and stretch the balls into very thin rounds.

If baked directly on stone in a very hot oven, the dough will acquire a perfect balance of crunch and tenderness in just a few minutes. At the edges, where there is no filling keeping it down, a crust will develop with beautiful alveoli. The filling itself should be modest and delicate as well. Adding too much sauce or cheese will make the pizza too heavy and soggy. Also, remember the filling should cook in just the same few minutes as required by the dough.

A wood-fired pizza oven can easily achieve temperatures of around 840°F to 930°F (450°C to 500°C). By keeping a few burning logs at the edges of the oven while baking it's possible to balance the baking of the crust and the toppings, creating an intense heat from both above and below. Baking at lower temperatures in a bakery or home oven is also possible, even though the baking might take slightly more time. In a home oven, you can preheat the baking stone to its maximum, and then choose to put it under the grill (for part of the time) while the pizza is in the oven, to provide sufficient heat from above as well. Or if you feel the topping of the pizza is baking too quickly and the crust stays too soft, use the grill to preheat the stone, and then turn it off while the pizza is in the oven.

Ingredients

pizza flour 450 grams
type T45 or T55; in the Italian coding: "00" or "0"
finely ground durum wheat semolina (*semola di grano duro rimacinata*) 50 grams (10%)
water 325-350 grams (65-70%)
salt 10 grams (2%)
yeast 2 grams (0.4%)
toppings of your choice

autolyse 45 minutes
kneading no kneading, except for the mixing of ingredients
weight of a dough piece as preferred, depending on the size of the pizza you would like to bake

These quantities are for five to six small pizzas; using a home oven it is usually easier to make several smaller pizzas rather than one big one

Method

Dough temperature after mixing and autolyse: 46°F to 50°F (8°C to 10°C); use literally ice-cold water and, during autolyse, place the dough back in the fridge. To mix, it is easiest to use a hand mixer with dough hooks.

Resting time (primary fermentation): overnight in the fridge (12 to 30 hours); the dough should be very airy and light, but still have some strength when touched and should hold its shape. To reinforce the dough, fold it once to three times, depending on the level of hydration you choose. If you feel the dough is not developing fast enough, remove it from the fridge three to six hours before baking.

Pré-façonnage: shape into small balls.

Resting time (proofing): either at room temperature or in the fridge, depending on your timing. Allow enough resting time for the dough to relax; as the balls will need to be rolled out and extended into very thin rounds, at least two hours are normally needed. You might also choose to make the balls in advance, the night before or in the morning, and then keep them in the fridge.

Shaping: use a rolling pin on a well-floured surface to extend the dough equally in all directions (turn the dough 90 degrees every time, rather than turning the rolling pin), try to avoid degassing the dough too much. Then do the final shaping by hand, continuing to turn the dough on the work surface, pulling it outwards slightly with every turn. Some pizza bakers let the dough hang off the work surface a little, letting gravity help a bit with extending the dough. Or lift the dough, putting your hands underneath, turning it, and extending it. Or, and this would be the most difficult method, make it spin in the air, again with your hands underneath.

The moment you feel the dough starts to be resistant, let it rest, if even for just a minute, otherwise the dough might pull back too much, tear, or become uneven (with thick parts and thin parts). On the other hand, don't let the dough become too extensible either, as it might easily become too thin, like a layer of filo dough.

Spread the sauce evenly over the pizza, using the back of a spoon, and add toppings. Leave the edges of the pizza uncovered. At all times, make sure the pizzas do not stick to the working surface, which should be sufficiently, but not excessively, floured.

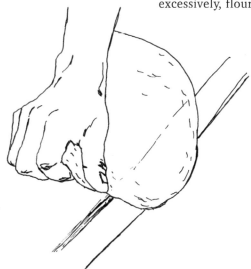

Baking

Lift the pizzas carefully and swiftly with a dough peel dusted with semolina flour. When baking at home you might choose to place baking parchment on the peel, and even add the toppings after the pizza has been placed on the baking parchment.

Baking in a stone oven: 570°F to 930°F (300°C to 500°C) (the standard for *pizza napoletana* is a temperature of 905°F (485°C) for the floor of the oven and 805°F (430°C) for the oven ceiling).

Baking at home with a baking stone: preheat the oven and stone to the highest temperature possible, even using the grill to heat the stone as well, but make sure that the oven itself does not get overheated.

Baking time: about 1.5 to 6 minutes or until the crust is well developed and has a good color and the filling is baked as well.

Fougasse

Fougasse is a bread from southern France with a large amount of crust, usually eaten with soups, salads, or a meal, breaking it rather than cutting it. It can be made plain, either with yeast or sourdough, or can be filled with fresh herbs such as sage, or with olive oil, olives, bacon, portobello mushrooms, or cheeses. In our bakery we make a plain sourdough *fougasse* but give it an extended development time so the flavor becomes relatively strong and pronounced. Here, I will give you two recipes to try, the one we use in the bakery on a daily basis, and one with yeast, olive oil and sage.

Sourdough fougasse

Two small changes in the procedure make this bread differ from the *batard*. The development time is extended to over 20 hours, making for a sudden increase in the acidity level, causing the bread to have a stronger and more pronounced flavor. Secondly, the bread is flattened and cut open on the inside just before baking, producing a crust to crumb ratio strongly favoring the crust. However, because no *grigne* is made, the crust will be chewy rather than crunchy.

These quantities are for two fougasses

Ingredients

bread flour 640 grams
type T65, medium strength
sourdough 320 grams (proportion flour to water: 1:1)
water 335-375 grams (together with the water in the sourdough 62-67%)
salt 16 grams (2%)

autolyse 45 minutes (flour, water, and sourdough)
kneading no kneading, except for the mixing of ingredients
weight of a dough piece about 650 grams

Method

Dough temperature after mixing and autolyse: 79°F (26°C).

Resting time (primary fermentation): about 2-3 hours at room temperature with one fold halfway; at the end the dough should feel airy.

Pré-façonnage: balls, followed by about 15 minutes resting.

Façonnage: shape into *batards*, taking special care to maintain adequate tension and to close the seam firmly.

Resting time (proofing): overnight in the fridge (18-22 hours); the *batards* should be airy, but still have some strength when touched. Because the dough will be cold, it will seem relatively firm.

Baking

Baking in a professional stone oven: 480°F (250°C), with moderate steam; open the valves after about 15 minutes, to ensure a dry environment for the last part of the baking.

Baking at home with a baking stone: preheat the oven and stone to the highest temperature possible; try to create ample steam, then bake at 430°F to 440°F (220°C to 230°C).

Scoring: do not score the bread, but flatten it just before baking, taking care not to degas too much. Then, with two sharp knives, cut right through the bread six times. Immediately open up the bread along the cuts, before the dough starts to reattach itself, or use a small dough scraper to press all the way through the dough to make the same cuts, see photo.

Baking time: about 25 minutes or until the crust is well developed and has a good color, and the bread is baked through.

Yeast fougasse with olive oil and sage

These quantities are for two fougasses

Because of the use of yeast, the flavor of the dough is less pronounced, and the flavors of the sage and olive oil will be more distinct. The recipe resembles the baguette recipe (*tradition*), but, like the sourdough *fougasse*, the dough is shaped first into a *batard*, then flattened and given its final shape using a dough cutter. As the dough rises well and will expand quite a lot, it is better to use a smaller amount of dough for the same size of *fougasse*. In other words, you keep the dough a bit thinner, expecting it to rise more in the oven.

Ingredients

bread flour 500 grams
type T65, medium strength)
water 340 grams (68%)
salt 10 grams (2%)
yeast 3.5 grams (0.7%)
olive oil 30 grams (6%)
fresh sage 10 grams (to taste)

autolyse 45 minutes (flour and water)
kneading no kneading, except for the mixing of ingredients
weight of a dough piece about 440 grams (two loaves)

Method

Dough temperature after mixing and autolyse: 75°F (24°C).

Let the sage sit in the oil for a while and then knead them both into the dough, after the yeast and the salt have been thoroughly mixed in.

Resting time (primary fermentation): about 1-2 hours at room temperature with one fold halfway or at least half an hour before shaping; at the end the dough should feel airy.

Pré-façonnage: balls, followed by about 15 minutes resting.

Façonnage: shape into batards, taking special care to maintain adequate tension.

Resting time (proofing): overnight in the fridge (18-22 hours); the batards should be airy, but still have some strength when touched. Because the dough will be cold, it will seem relatively firm.

Baking

Baking in a professional stone oven: 480°F (250°C), with moderate steam; open the valves after about 15 minutes, to ensure a dry environment for the last part of the baking.

Baking at home with a baking stone: preheat the oven and stone to the highest temperature possible; try to create ample steam, then bake at 430°F (220°C) but if necessary, further reduce the temperature to 375°F (190°C) after about 10 minutes.

Scoring and baking time: like the sourdough *fougasse* (see page 181).

Pain de mie
and pain brié

Pain de mie, "bread of the crumb", is the opposite of the other types of bread promoted in this book. It's typically the kind of bread you would find in a supermarket (or traditional bakery) in many countries, including the UK, the U.S., and Canada, but also more and more in France. It is characterized by lightness and a relatively large volume, while having a very fine crumb without any large alveoli. Often, flavor development is minimal. It's ideal for toasting.

Despite the departure from the characteristics of the other bread in this book, there is value in learning to make *pain de mie*. It will teach you about the effects that intensive kneading, forceful shaping and rapid development have on bread. And if you attempt to store this bread and prevent it from becoming stale you will discover why commercial bakeries commonly use so many preservatives.

And yet, just a few modifications to the procedures can produce a far better bread, with qualities of its own, combining lightness and a soft crust with flavor. *Pain de mie* with an extended proofing is well suited for baking with grains other than wheat. You can substitute part of the wheat flour for buckwheat, oat flour, rye, or quinoa. As the bread is baked in a tin, it will become denser but will not flatten.

A number of traditional breads are made in the fashion of *pain de mie*. Here we provide one of those recipes, as adapted by one of our bakers and known as *pain brié*. He in turn learned the recipe from his father, who was also a baker. The recipe originates in Normandy, where it is known as "sailor's bread", meant to stay fresh on trips out to sea.

Photo: pain brié, sailor's bread from Normandy, recipe on page 190

Classic pain de mie

These quantities are for one pain de mie

Ingredients

bread flour 500 grams
type for example T55, strong or medium strength
cold water 300 grams (60%)
salt 10 grams (2%)
yeast 3.5 to 7 grams (0.67 - 1.33%)

autolyse none
kneading intensive kneading
weight of a dough piece about 800 grams

Method

Dough temperature after mixing and autolyse: 81°F (27°C). Mix the yeast into the flour, then add water and salt, mix on a low speed in a dough machine for 5 minutes, then at high speed for 10 minutes, or until the dough detaches from the sides of the mixing bowl and can be stretched into a very thin film. Be careful that the dough doesn't go beyond this point, as overmixing will break down the gluten again, making the dough shiny and weak. When kneading by hand, knead well and with force, until a similar point is reached (although its development will usually be slightly less than can be achieved with a dough machine, unless you are very patient and keep on kneading and kneading...).

Resting time (primary fermentation): about 30 minutes to 1 hour at room temperature; at the end, the dough should feel airy and have doubled in size.

Pré-façonnage: none.

Façonnage: degas and fold and shape into rolls, applying force and repeating the folding and closing of the seam several times, while continuing to exert pressure on the dough pieces to degas them. Place into an oiled baking tin for bread, preferably with a lid.

Resting time (proofing): 30 minutes to 1 hour, or until the dough has doubled in size.

Baking

Baking in a professional rotary oven: 430°F (220°C), with moderate steam; open the valves after about 30 minutes and take the lid off the tin.

Baking at home (in a baking tin on an oven rack): preheat the oven to 430°F (220°C), try, if you are not using a lid, to create ample steam; do not use a baking stone; remove the lid of the baking tin after about 25 minutes.

Scoring: do not score the bread.

Baking time: bake for about 40 minutes or until the crust is golden, and the bread is baked through.

You can bake pain de mie either in a tin with a lid and without steaming, or in a tin without a lid and ample steam

Pain de mie with slow fermentation

(any kind of flour)

These quantities are for one pain de mie

As with the baguette tradition, you can also give this bread a shorter primary fermentation and a longer proofing. However, this will increase the chances of larger alveoli in the final bread and will cause the crust to form small blisters that are normally not associated with pain de mie.

Ingredients

bread flour 500 grams
type for example T55, medium strength
cold water 300 grams – adapt when using wholemeal flour or other kinds of grains (60%)
salt 10 grams (2%)
yeast 1 gram (0,2%)

autolyse 45 minutes
kneading light kneading
weight of a dough piece about 800 grams

Method

Dough temperature after mixing and autolyse: 64°F (18°C). Just mix the ingredients, using autolyse, then keep on kneading for a few more minutes. It is not necessary to reach full dough development yet. If you try to stretch a piece of dough into a thin film, it may still tear easily.

Resting time (primary fermentation): about 10 to 15 hours in the fridge, with one fold half way, to degas the dough; at the end the dough should feel airy.

Façonnage: degas and fold and shape into rolls, applying force and repeating the folding and closing of the seam several times, while continuing to exert pressure on the dough pieces to degas them. Place in an oiled baking tin for bread, preferably one with a lid.

Resting time (proofing): one hour at room temperature, or until the dough has doubled in size.

Baking

The bread is baked in the same way as the regular *pain de mie* (see page 187).

Pain brié (sailor's bread from Normandie)

These quantities are for one pain brié

Photo pain brié: page 185

Recipe adapted by Charlie de Saint Jores

A pâte fermentée is an old dough, already fermented. It can be made especially for the occasion (ideally the day before, letting it develop slowly, but if necessary, also just a few hours before by using more yeast or increasing the dough temperature) or it can be a piece of leftover dough (as would be the practice in most bakeries using the method). To make a pâte fermentée, all you need to do is just mix the ingredients.

Ingredients

bread flour 300 grams
type T55 or T65, medium strength
pâte fermentée 300 grams (187 grams flour, 60% water, 2% salt, 0.33% yeast)
water 100 grams (together with the water in the *pâte fermentée*: 43.5%)
water temperature cold if kneading with a dough mixer, at room temperature if kneading by hand
unsalted butter 75 grams (15% of the total flour weight)
salt 6 grams (2% of flour in the dough)
yeast 0.6 grams (0.2% of flour in the dough)

autolyse none
kneading well kneaded
weight of a dough piece about 800 grams

Method

Dough temperature after mixing and autolyse: 75°F (24°C). Mix the *pâte fermentée*, flour, water, salt, and yeast, until the flour is completely hydrated. Then keep on kneading for at least 10 more minutes. Knead in the butter. The dough is very firm, and it is normal that a lot of effort is required to knead it properly. Do not use a hand mixer as the dough will put too much strain on it.

Resting time (primary fermentation): about two hours at room temperature, with one fold halfway (or just rounding the dough). Do not use flour when working the dough, just slightly moist hands.

Pré-façonnage: balls, followed by about five minutes resting.

Façonnage: degas and shape into a *batard*, using ample force. Repeat the steps of folding and closing the seam a number of times while continuing to put pressure on the dough to make sure it is properly degassed, until the dough piece reaches its maximum tension. The last time, take special care to close the seam firmly.

Resting time (proofing): one hour at room temperature, or until the dough has doubled in size.

Baking

Baking in a professional stone oven: 430°F (220°C), with moderate steam; open the valves after about 30 minutes to ensure a dry environment towards the end of baking. If possible, set the floor temperature of the oven to 410°F (210°C) and the top temperature at 440°F (230°C).

Baking at home with a baking stone: preheat the oven to its maximum to heat up the stone and then bake at 410°F (210°C); try to create ample steam.

Scoring: egg wash the bread and score just before baking, making deep straight cuts from one end of the loaf to the other, all at the same angle, starting with a cut right through the center.

Baking time: bake about 40 minutes or until the crust is golden, and the bread is baked through.

Stollen

Stollen is bread made in Holland and Germany for Easter and Christmas. It's made with a very rich dough, containing milk, butter, eggs, fruits, and nuts. Often, though not always, the bread is filled with almond paste as well. In many respects, a good *stollen* is more like a pastry than a bread.

We make our own almond paste in our bakery. And unless you live in one of those countries where almonds are always excellent and any respectable pastry shop will make a very nice almond paste for you on request, it might be best to make it yourself as well. Commercially available almond paste, as can sometimes be bought in wholesale shops and is used by many bakers, is often of very poor quality. The fewer almonds used, the more sugar and sometimes even beans, the cheaper its production – not to mention the artificial flavors used to pretend that the almonds were of good quality. However, making your own almond paste does require some planning and thinking ahead. It's a very simple recipe, but it needs to stand for at least two weeks, and preferably longer.

You also need to do some planning with regard to the preparation of the fruit mixture – this also gets better if you leave it to stand for a few days. You will get the best results if you let the fruit soak in dark rum. The flavor will improve, but also the fruit will become moister through absorbing the rum, and this in turn will help to keep the bread moister too – it will stay fresh longer. The alcohol in the rum also protects the fruit, and in turn the bread, from mold, allowing you to keep the bread for up to two weeks. Be aware that alcohol fumes are emitted while you mix it with the fruit, and while the dough proofs. Considering the large quantities we make in the bakery, it is easy to accidentally get a little drunk on fumes while working...

Ingredients

The almond paste can be used after four or five days but the flavor will improve further if you leave the paste to stand for longer. Under proper hygienic standards, the dough can be kept refrigerated for about three months.

700 grams of almond paste will be used for the filling in this recipe, for seven stollen

Almond paste – two weeks in advance
high quality blanched almonds 350 grams
finely ground sugar or castor sugar 250 grams
eggs 2
lemon zest of 2 lemons
lemon juice of 2 lemons

Fruit mixture – two days before starting the dough
currants 200 grams
sultana raisins 700 grams, white and dark mixed
dried figs 100 grams, cut into small pieces
zest of 2 oranges
dark rum 150 grams
together 115% of the flour weight!

The percentages in the poolish and the dough are always in relation to the total flour weight

Poolish – the day before starting the dough
flour 250 grams (25%)
type "gruau" T55 or T65, strong white flour
cold milk 250 grams (25%)
yeast 7 grams (0.7%)

Dough
bread flour 750 grams (75%)
type T55 or T65, medium strength or strong
blanched almonds 200 grams, lightly roasted (20%)
sugar 40 grams (4%)
milk 75 grams (7.5%, together with poolish 32.5%)
water 165 grams (16.5%)
egg 135 grams, or 2 very large eggs (13.5%)
salt 20 grams (2%)
yeast 10 grams (1%; together with poolish 1.7%)
butter 200 grams (20%)
cinnamon 10 grams (4%)

These quantities are
for seven stollen

autolyse 20 minutes (flour, sugar, poolish, milk, water, and eggs)
kneading some kneading, not too intensive
weight of a dough piece about 450 grams

Method

To make the almond paste

Roast $1/3$ of the almonds in the oven at 320°F (160°C) until well colored, golden, but not overdone (they will become bitter) and leave to cool.

Using a food processor, roughly grind all the almonds (roasted and unroasted), using pulses to avoid heating up the almonds too much. They should not become oily. If you are making a larger quantity, like in this recipe, it is best to grind the almonds in batches. Mix in the sugar, and grind everything together for a second time, this time more finely. Stop just before the almonds are getting too fine and start lumping together (the almond texture should be retained for almond paste; if you were to continue too long you would reach the fine structure of marzipan).

Mix in ½ of the lemon juice, ½ of the lemon zest and one of the two eggs. Add some (or all) of the remaining lemon zest and/or lemon juice to taste. If it remains too dry add some (or all) of the second egg as well. You want it to be a strong paste, workable like clay, but bear in mind that the almonds will absorb a bit more liquid when the paste is left to stand, so the paste can still be slightly on the moist side at this point. The lemon juice makes the paste taste fresher, but if too much is used, may make it sour. The zest makes the taste fuller but can produce a bitter flavor if too much is used. Leave to stand in the fridge for at least one week, preferably longer. If well preserved, the almond paste will keep for up to three months.

To make the fruit mixture

Mix all the fruit, the orange zest and rum, and leave to stand for at least one night, preferably two or three. Stir the mixture once in between, to make sure the rum is evenly absorbed by the fruit. The fruit mixture can be kept for up to two weeks.

Poolish

Mix flour and cold milk with a hand mixer until all the flour is hydrated. Leave to stand for half an hour and mix in the yeast, sprinkling it over finely to avoid lumps. Put in the fridge overnight. If you do not have the time, leave it to stand at room temperature until well fermented: 2 to 4 hours.

Dough

Dough temperature after mixing: 75°F to 81°F (24°C to 27°C). After autolyse, mix in the salt and yeast and knead for a few minutes with a mixer, or for up to ten minutes if working by hand. The gluten structure should be quite developed, but not fully yet. Mix in the butter and knead until well absorbed. Add the cinnamon to the fruit mixture, and stir well, then mix into the dough. Finally, mix in the almonds.

Resting time (primary fermentation): two hours at room temperature, with one fold in between. Towards the end, the dough should feel airy, but will not necessarily have doubled in size.

Pré-façonnage: balls; be careful not to tear the dough but also be careful not to use too much flour. Let them stand for 10 to 14 minutes. While the dough pieces rest, prepare the almond paste filling: make seven rolls of 100 grams, about 15 cm long.

Façonnage: flatten and lengthen the balls slightly and then shape into *batards*, placing the almond rolls on the inside of the dough, incorporating them lengthwise in the first "fold" (see photos on page 198). Make sure you close the seam very well at the end.

Resting time (proofing): leave the bread for about two hours at room temperature. The loaves should already start to feel a little airy when pressed (in between the almonds) but should still have ample force. Then leave overnight in the fridge (12 to 16 hours), until airy and one and a half times their original size. When touched (in between the almonds) the dough should give way easily, and only slowly return to its original shape. If you are in a hurry, it is also possible to do a shorter proofing at room temperature. The rich filling will compensate for the lesser flavor development of the dough although the bread will keep for less time.

Baking

Baking in a professional stone oven: on a baking tray, 390°F (200°C), with ample steam; open the valves after about 30 minutes, to ensure a dry environment for the last part of the baking. After the first 15 minutes, slowly let the temperature fall to 355°F (180°C).

Baking at home on a baking tray: preheat the oven to 430°F (220°C); try to create ample steam; lower the temperature to 390°F (200°C) as soon as the bread is in the oven. After 15 minutes, lower the temperature to 355°F (180°C).

Scoring: do not score before baking and make sure the seam is at the bottom.

Baking time: bake about 40-50 minutes or until the bread is baked through; due to the sugars in the dough, the color of the crust will tend to be on the dark side.

If the bread tears during baking, it means that either the bread wasn't sufficiently developed before baking, or humidity in the oven wasn't sufficient. If the seam opens up, it means that it was either not well closed, not at the bottom of the bread, or again, that the bread wasn't sufficiently developed.

Brioche

Brioche is an extremely rich dough, but without a filling. In France, brioches are made both by bread bakers and by pastry shops. It is rich to the extent of being cake-like, but as it contains yeast as a raising agent, it also qualifies as a bread dough. A good brioche has a markedly light texture, and a very rich, full flavor. It can be eaten fresh or toasted and can be baked as individual small rolls (usually *"brioche à tête"*, small buns with a "head") or as larger loaves (either huge *brioche à tête*, or in the shape of a typical *pain de mie* baked in a baking mold, ideal for slicing and toasting). In many ways, it is similar to the Italian *pan d'oro,* which normally would be made with a light sourdough rather than yeast.

Usually, brioche dough is kneaded extensively and intensively, thus creating the typical light and airy structure, but this method also severely compromises flavor, and together with a more rapid proofing, causes the brioche to be rather dry and often insipid. The eggs in the dough tend to make the brioche dry out relatively quickly anyway, making a longer dough development all the more necessary to achieve a good result. Also, one might wonder, why use all those eggs, if the dough is subsequently kneaded to such an extent that the eggs lose their color and flavor?

The recipe below provides an example of how to make a very rich dough, achieve an airy and very fine crumb, without compromising flavor or keeping qualities. To achieve this result, autolyse is all the more important. The use of a poolish provides proper acidity and flavor from fermentation, before eggs, butter, and sugar are added in such quantities that the yeast is actually slowed down.

These quantities are for 25-30
small *brioches à tête* or two
large brioche loaves

*The percentages in the poolish and the
dough are always in relation to the total
flour weight*

Ingredients

Poolish – approximately one hour before starting the dough
flour 125 grams (25%)
type T55 or T65 gruau, strong white flour
cold milk 75 grams (15%)
yeast 5.5 grams (1.1%)

Dough
flour 375 grams (75%)
type T55 or T65 gruau, strong white flour
sugar 60 grams (12%)
egg 225 grams, ± 4 to 5 eggs, directly from the fridge (45%)
salt 12 grams (2.4%)
butter 225 grams, at room temperature, cut into small pieces
so it can easily be incorporated into the dough (45%)
egg 1, for egg wash

autolyse 45 minutes (flour, sugar, poolish, eggs)
kneading some kneading, not too intensive
weight of a dough piece depending on the size of the molds
used, a small individual *brioche à tête* might need just 40
grams of dough

Method

Poolish
Mix the flour and yeast, then add the cold milk and mix
using a hand mixer, a fork, or your hands until all the flour is
hydrated (normally, even when starting with a hand mixer or
fork, it might be necessary to finish off mixing by hand, using
some force, as otherwise it will be difficult to incorporate all
of the flour). Leave to stand at room temperature until well
developed, soft, and airy; this usually takes about one and a
half to two hours.

Dough
Start about 45 minutes before the poolish is fully developed, or
about 45 minutes after starting the poolish, to be on the safe

side. Of course, the first time this is a wild guess, and it is good to know that leaving it slightly longer will only have a positive effect on the final dough quality.

Mix the flour, sugar and egg until the flour is hydrated. Leave to stand for 45 minutes, or until the poolish is well developed. The dough temperature after mixing should be as cold as possible.

When the poolish is at its peak and feels very airy, mix it in to the dough together with the salt and knead for four minutes on low speed with a planetary dough mixer, a bit longer in a spiral mixer, or up to ten or fifteen minutes if working by hand. The gluten structure should be quite developed, but not fully yet. Mix in the butter; if using a dough mixer first mix in roughly by hand, to avoid the butter sticking to the sides of the bowl and taking much more time to be incorporated. Knead until the butter is fully incorporated and evenly distributed. This should take roughly three to five minutes; if using a planetary mixer, you might have to scrape the hook or the sides of the bowl in between to incorporate the dough that has stuck onto them.

Be careful not to overwork and thus overheat the dough, as this will only make the butter softer and softer. The dough will become sticky and will appear to be underdeveloped, whereas in fact it has been worked too much. If it really takes more than a few minutes to incorporate the butter, it means it should have been mixed in better by hand first, or that the butter was still too cold. As soon as the dough is ready, place it overnight in the fridge in an airtight container.

Resting time (primary fermentation): overnight in the fridge (the dough can be kept at this stage for up to three days); the dough does not need to be folded; do not let it rise at room temperature towards the end, leave it in the fridge until it is airy and has at least doubled in size.

Pré-façonnage: shape into balls for small individual brioches; work quickly so that the dough doesn't have a chance to come to room temperature and become sticky. If making larger, *pain de mie*-type brioche baked in tins, pre-shape into a roll as for a baguette.

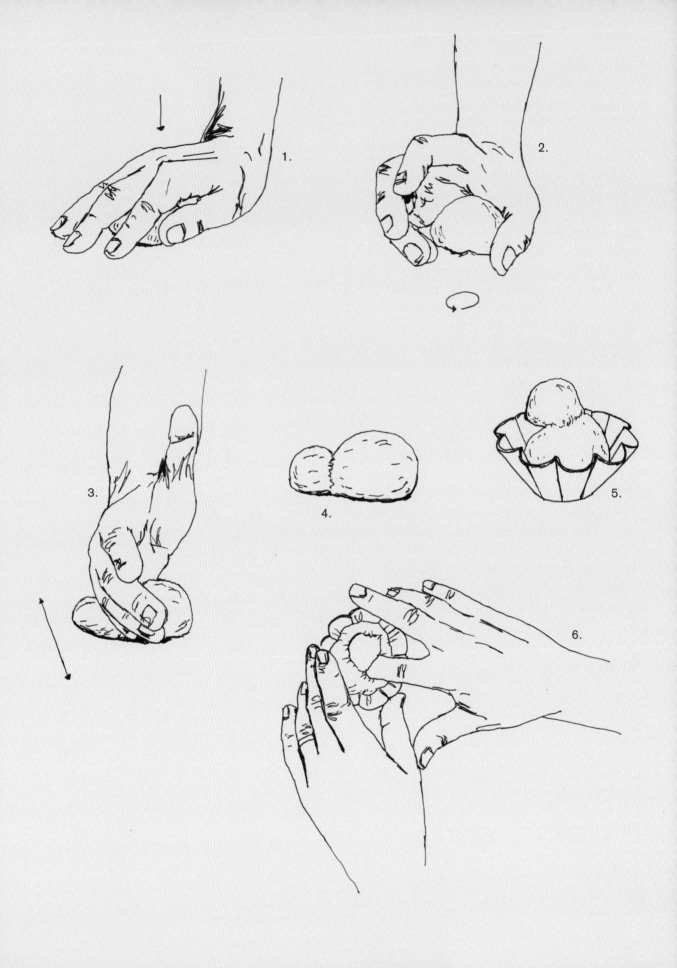

1.

2.

3.

4.

5.

6.

Façonnage: when making a large brioche loaf, shape it again into a roll, in the same way as you would for a *pain de mie*, pressing the air out of the dough and repeating the folding and closing movements over and over until maximum tension is reached. You can then bake the brioches in a baking tin just like for a *pain de mie*. To make small individual brioches, place the little balls sideways on a floured work surface, and make an indent with the side of your hand by rolling at the two thirds mark until you almost cut through the dough, thus creating the head. Place in a lightly oiled baking mold with the head up and press down alongside the head with your fingertips until you almost reach the bottom of the mold. Without this last step the brioche will return to its original ball-like shape while baking.

Resting time (proofing): at room temperature until doubled in size (usually about two hours). When pressed, the dough should feel very light and airy, but still retain a very light springiness, returning slowly to its original shape. The brioche can also be frozen at this stage and be kept in the freezer for up to three days (if kept longer, the flavor will slowly change, and the yeast will become less active when baking). In this case, take the brioche out about twenty minutes before baking, and egg wash them after taking them out of the freezer, rather than before freezing them.

Baking

Baking in a professional stone oven: in the tins on a baking tray, 390°F (200°C), without steam. If possible, choose a somewhat higher temperature for the top of the oven.

Baking at home: preheat the oven to about 375°F (190°C). Place the molds on a baking tray, do not create steam.

Scoring: do not score, but egg wash carefully just before baking.

Baking time: bake for about 12 minutes for small individual brioche, or until golden and just baked (baking too long will cause the brioche to dry out too much). For larger breads, adjust the time according to the size chosen. If the brioche bread bakes too quickly, turn the temperature down.

Challah

Challah is a traditional Jewish bread, made with an enriched dough often containing eggs, sugar or honey, and usually oil but sometimes butter. It is traditionally eaten after the sabbath. The reason for including it here, as the final recipe, is that apart from having a very tender structure and pleasing flavor, it is a braided bread. The recipe thus enables you to try one more technique.

Very often, even in France and Italy, braided bread or bread rolls are made with a very insipid "milk dough", easy to work with, easy to bake, shiny because it is egg washed, but absolutely flavorless. Traditional *challah,* however, proves that it is not necessary to work this way. You can have your cake and eat it too, as the bread is both pleasing to the eye and enjoyable to eat. It's also an example of a *pain de mie* recipe which has been improved with an extended proofing time, giving it much better keeping qualities and more flavor.

The recipe below is made using a poolish. It is also possible to make dough directly (without a starter) but with a lengthened proofing in the refrigerator. You can vary it in many other ways too: oil or butter, more or less egg. My personal preference is for just a little bit of egg, and the recipe has been written accordingly. If you want to use more eggs, for example two or three, then you need to adjust the water percentage: about 50 grams less water for every egg that is added. Autolyse can be skipped if you are pressed for time, but in that case, kneading time needs to be lengthened. You can also speed up the recipe by adding a little more yeast. The bread flavor will be slightly less pronounced and delicate, but the added ingredients still ensure a flavorful loaf that keeps well.

Ingredients

These quantities are for
one large challah

*The percentages in the poolish and the
dough are always in relation to the total
flour weight*

Poolish — the day before
flour 100 grams (20%)
type T55 or T65 medium strength
cold water 100 grams cold (20%)
yeast 1 gram (0.2%)

Dough
flour 400 grams (80%)
type T55 or T65 medium strength
water 150 grams (50%; together with the water in the poolish)
honey 50 grams (10%)
egg 50 grams, ± 1 medium egg, at room temperature (10%)
salt 10 grams (2%)
yeast 2 grams (0.4%)
vegetable oil or butter 50 grams, butter at room temperature, cut into small chunks so it can easily be incorporated into the dough (10%)
egg 1, for the egg wash
poppyseeds or sesame seeds, optional

autolyse 20 minutes (poolish, flour, water, honey, and egg)
kneading medium kneading
weight of a dough piece 900 grams

Method

Poolish
Mix flour and yeast, add water, and mix with a fork or hand mixer until all the flour is hydrated. Place the poolish in the fridge. Before using, the poolish should be well developed and bubbly. For a speedier process, it is also possible to make the poolish with lukewarm water and then keep it at room temperature.

Dough
Dough temperature after mixing and autolyse: 75°F (24°C). Mix the poolish, flour, water, honey, and egg and knead for about three minutes by hand or one minute at low speed with a planetary mixer. Then let it stand for 20 minutes before mixing

in first the salt and then the yeast. Knead for about 5 to 10 minutes until the gluten structure is well developed, but not fully. Knead in the butter or oil, until well incorporated. Place the dough into a lightly greased container as soon as it is ready and cover it with plastic wrap or a damp dishtowel.

Resting time (primary fermentation): at room temperature for about three hours, with two folds in between, one after an hour, one after two hours. Towards the end, the dough should feel airy and have doubled in size.

Pré-façonnage: the number of dough pieces you cut depends on the kind of braid you would like to make. To make a three-strand braid, cut three pieces of 300 grams each, and for a six-strand braid, six pieces of 150 grams each. Pre-shape each dough piece into a ball and then leave them to rest.

Façonnage: first shape the balls into small *batards*, then allow to rest before rolling them into strands about 40 centimeters long, as if shaping very thin baguettes. If the dough is too springy, give it a little extra rest midway through the rolling. Then braid the strands together; the example shown here is of a six-strand braid. Lay all the ends together on one side and press the tips together. At the other end, fan the strands out a little, so you make a triangle shape. Take one of the outside strands and place it in the center. Then take the second strand on the opposite side and cross it over the rest, all the way over. Now take the outside strand on the opposite side and place in the center, while taking hold of the second-most outside strand on the other side at the end and crossing it all the way over. Continue like this until the braid is completed, press the ends together and fold them a little bit under the dough, so the braid is closed. Place the braided loaf on a sheet of baking parchment on a baking tray or a peel, and brush with egg wash.

The illustrations are on page 210

Resting time (proofing): about one to two hours, until the loaf has doubled in volume. When you press it with your finger, it should still slowly regain its original shape. Pay close attention, if the bread has had either too little or too much proofing the braid can lose its shape while baking.

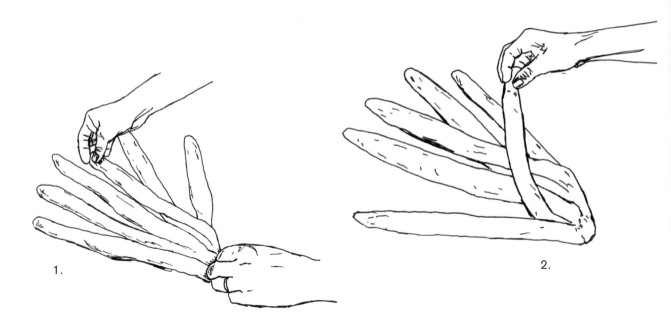

1.

2.

Baking

Baking in a professional stone oven: 375°F (190°C), no steam; open the valves after about 20 minutes. Let the temperature of the oven drop to 340°F (170°C) after the first 10 minutes. Take care that the loaf doesn't color too quickly and, if necessary, further adjust the temperature while baking.

Baking at home on a baking tray: 340°F (170°C), making sure that the bread doesn't color too quickly and, if necessary, adjusting the temperature.

Baking at home with a baking stone: preheat the oven to its maximum to heat up the stone and then bake at 340°F (170°C), making sure that the bread doesn't color too quickly and, if necessary, adjusting the temperature.

Scoring: do not score, but egg wash the bread once more just before baking; sprinkle with sesame or poppyseeds if you like.

Baking time: bake about 35-40 minutes or until the crust is golden, and the bread is baked right through.

Making your
own choices

Making your own choices

By now you will have a basic understanding of what happens in a dough, as well as some experience. This chapter, by offering you a list of examples of common "causes and effects", provides you with some clues for how to adjust recipes, and how to reach the specific quality you may be looking for in the bread you are baking.

Having tried a number of the recipes above, but especially having tried to understand what happens to the doughs and loaves passing through your hands, you will find that the recipes themselves become less and less useful. In fact, the recipes will turn out to be inadequate. Depending on the circumstances, the characteristics of the flour, the temperature in the bakery or at home, the oven you use, and your own timing, you will want to modify or adjust them. You obviously still need to carefully weigh flour, salt, and yeast or sourdough; you may need to further improve your basic skills in shaping; you will need to choose (and find) the flour you want to use. But most importantly, you will need to choose the kind of bread you want to bake, to set the goal you want to achieve.

It might sound difficult to make your own recipes or adjust existing ones. Just try though, and then judge. Start off by not taking it too seriously and see what happens. To help you get started, I will summarize some of the main variables to consider.

To achieve an open structure and irregular alveoli...

- be sure to use a proper bread flour
- use light flour (between type 45 and 80)
- use a more liquid dough
- use a more liquid sourdough
- use autolyse
- knead less and allow more time for the dough to develop, use folding as a means of giving it the required strength, but don't fold too often
- exert little pressure when weighing or shaping the dough, thus avoiding degassing the dough pieces
- ensure that the dough pieces reach sufficient surface tension during shaping
- ensure that the primary fermentation is sufficient, and that the shaped loaf still has enough power to "explode" in the oven after proofing, i.e. is *almost* fully developed
- bake directly on the floor of the oven, or on a baking stone, or in a well pre-heated cast-iron pot
- start baking at a relatively high temperature, then, if necessary, let the temperature drop
- use sufficient (but not excessive) steam

To increase the volume of the bread...

- be sure to use a proper bread flour
- use a white flour, e.g. type 45, 55 or 65
- use a more intensive or prolonged kneading process
- allow sufficient time for the primary fermentation if the dough is not to be kneaded extensively
- use autolyse
- degas the dough when weighing and shaping
- ensure that the dough pieces reach sufficient surface tension when shaping
- bake directly on the floor of the oven
- use sufficient (but not excessive) steam

To increase the strength of a dough and facilitate shaping...

- knead the dough to a sufficient level of development, or allow enough time for the primary fermentation phase
- use the technique of folding one or more times during the primary fermentation phase; the more liquid a dough, the more folding might be required
- add less water if you feel the dough is properly developed but sticky
- add more water if you feel the dough remains weak due to not developing quickly enough

To make a beautiful grigne...

- be sure the dough is not too weak (e.g. due to very high hydration, too much acidity, a lack of development, or over-development)
- ensure that the dough pieces have enough surface tension while shaping, especially if you allow a long time for the proofing phase (e.g. by placing the shaped loaves in the fridge overnight)
- let the shaped dough pieces rest in baskets or between the layers of a *couche*, so that some support is provided
- bake directly on the floor of the oven or on a baking stone
- use a very sharp *lame* to score the bread just before baking, and don't score too deeply
- use sufficient steam, more when the dough is less developed, less when the dough is more developed

To strengthen the crust...

- knead less, and allow a longer time for the fermentation and proofing of the dough (either before or after shaping, or both)
- use very little yeast, or use a sourdough
- don't bake at too high a temperature, or let the temperature decrease while baking
- bake directly on the oven floor, or on a baking stone, or in a heavy baking tin with a lid
- keep the oven moist for an appropriate time while baking. Only allow the steam to escape completely from the oven towards the end of baking and not before that time

To make the crust thinner...

- knead more, and allow less time for the fermentation and proofing of the dough, e.g. increase the temperature or the amount of yeast; especially avoid an overnight development of the dough
- avoid the use of sourdough
- if available, use flour with a relatively high amount of amylase
- bake on a baking tray or in a light baking tin
- bake at a higher temperature
- use sufficient steam at the beginning of baking, but ensure that the oven is dry as soon as the bread gets some color

To make a thin but crunchy crust...

- use yeast, but not too much
- use flour with a relatively high amylase content
- find a balance between sufficient time for amylase to create sugars in the dough, and too much time, causing the creation of acids; choose a dough temperature which is not too high so that the creation of sugars slightly outruns the use of sugars by the yeast
- make sure the *grigne* opens well: this will actually be the part of the bread which will give the crunchy sensation while eating

To achieve a fuller flavor...

- knead as little as possible
- give the dough a long time to develop, either before or after shaping, or both, at a relatively low temperature for at least part of the time
- use very little yeast, or a sourdough, or a starter dough
- weigh and shape by hand, without degassing the dough
- make sure the development level is sufficient, especially before shaping
- make sure there is sufficient humidity in the oven during the first stage of baking, so the crust can develop, and let the bread cool down properly before cutting

To achieve a crumb which stays fresh longer...

- knead a bit more
- give the dough a long time to develop, either before or after shaping, or both
- use very little yeast, or a sourdough, or a starter dough
- make the dough moister
- make sure the crust develops well while baking

To vary the level and kind of acidity and flavor...

- degassing the dough while shaping it will cause volatile flavor agents to be removed from the dough while acids remain, causing the final bread to have a much more pronounced acidic flavor and taste saltier
- the more liquid and airier the sourdough and the dough, the more lactic acid bacteria will dominate, thus creating less of an acidic flavor; and vice versa, the denser and more compact, the more acetic acid bacteria will dominate, creating more pronounced acidity
- the longer the proofing time, the more acidic the bread will be
- using less sourdough can create a more acidic bread, if the development of the bread is too slow

Appendix

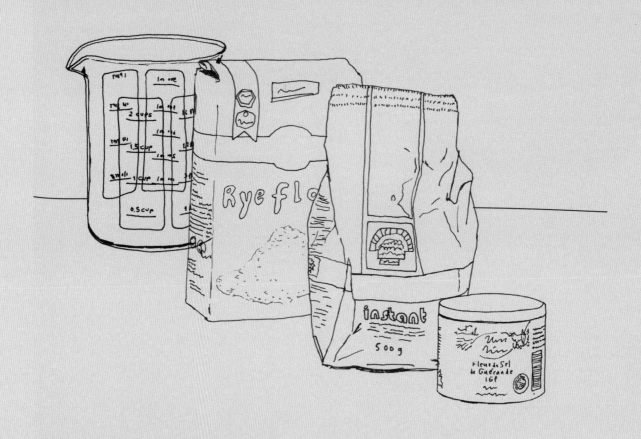

Glossary of French and other baking terms

Alveoli
The holes or bubbles of "air" found inside bread

Autolyse
A rest period given to a dough just after mixing, before any kneading takes place and before salt or yeast are added

Biga
A relatively dry starter dough

Couche
Linen cloth on which the bread is left to rest and proof after shaping

Façonnage
The shaping of the bread; sometimes specified as *pré-façonnage*, the pre-shaping or initial shaping, and *façonnage*, the final shaping

Gluten
The strings of protein inside a dough, that hold back the gases it contains

Grigne
The place where the bread has opened up while baking

Lame
The very sharp razor used to cut dough just before baking

Levain
Sourdough, emphasis in the word is on leavening power, not on acidity

Pâte fermentée
A starter dough consisting of a portion of the final dough, which is made in advance

Paton
A piece of dough for a single bread, shaped or unshaped

Peel
A tool for transferring dough into or out of the oven when baking directly on stone

Poolish
A relatively moist starter dough

Primary fermentation
The "bulk" development of a dough before it is divided into pieces for *façonnage*

Proofing
The development of dough pieces after *façonnage*

Starter
A bit of dough that is made in advance and later added to the final dough

The technical characteristics and qualities of flour

Addressing this issue is most relevant if you are able to acquire information about the chemical and physical nature of the flour you are using. This is not always the case, even in professional baking, and then you are left to test the various flours or flour brands you have at your disposal by baking to find out what works best. Still, it is good to know the differences between various flours so it will be easier to understand what could be the cause of a flour, or consequently a dough, behaving in a certain way. With experience, you will be able to partly understand the technical specifications of a certain flour just by using it, even if the information is not available from your supermarket or mill.

W or strength

"W" stands for the strength of the gluten which can be developed when adding water to flour and kneading it. It is measured by taking a piece of dough, made according to a fixed standard, containing flour and salted water, and blowing it up as if it were a balloon.

An average bread flour nowadays has a strength expressed as a W-value of 180-220; "weaker" flours are below 180, while "strong" flour would have a 'W' of 220 or more. Strong flours are especially suitable for filled doughs, such as those heavy with fruit, like *stollen*, or heavy with butter, milk, and eggs, like brioche. The gluten will be strong enough to lift the filling and will not tear as easily when fillings such as nuts – with sharp edges – are added. When used for regular bread, a strong flour can aid in developing a very open structure, with large alveoli, as the gluten can retain more gases. The crust might also become stronger and sometimes less *croustilliant* as strong flours tend to absorb more water as well. The kneading time might have to be adjusted too, as the flour takes more time to reach its optimal strength. On the other hand, a weak flour might result in a bread with little volume that does not hold its shape (although the extensibility and elasticity of the gluten are also crucial for this, see below).

In the past, flours generally used to be weaker. Through selective cultivation, grains have been developed to produce stronger flour. There are also regional differences, due to soil, climate, and local varieties in wheat types. In the US and Canada, relatively "strong" flours are more common than in Europe. In Italy, a specific kind of grain used for the production of pasta, called *grano duro* (strong, durum wheat), is also used for some varieties of bread, after it has been ground more finely (*rimacinata*). This is not just a strong wheat flour, however, but a different species of wheat, also containing a large quantity of broken starches which can easily be converted into sugars by the amylase enzymes. So, adding a small proportion of this flour into a bread dough can result in more crustiness, as well as a specific flavor and yellowish color characteristic of the durum wheat itself.

Falling number or amylase

The "falling number" of flour refers to its enzymatic activity, most specifically the amount and activity of the amylase enzyme which turns starches into sugars. The quicker this process works, the sooner the starches will be broken down. This is tested by heating a test tube filled with a suspension of flour and water until the starches turn into jelly. The thickness and resistance of the jelly are subsequently measured by measuring the time it takes, in seconds, for the jelly to fall down in the test setting: the "falling number". Thus, the higher the number, the more time it took for the enzymes to develop their activity. A high falling number thus expresses a weak flour in terms of its amylase activity, while a low falling number represents a very high concentration of amylase.

A low concentration of amylase will cause the dough to develop slowly, as the sugars created by its activity are not sufficient for the yeast to work at its best (remember the yeast needs sugar to convert it into gases and alcohols). In such a case, take care not to use too much yeast and increase development times. This will bring the relative paces of both processes (the working of the yeast and the working of the amylase) into balance again. A different approach to a relatively slow flour is to increase the hydration level of the dough. This helps to speed up the enzymatic process, as there is more "free" water available for the amylase enzyme to metabolize.

When using sourdough, it may be difficult to find the right balance, and if the activity is really too low, bread may become sour, precisely because of the slowed-down development. Too high a concentration of amylase will cause the dough to weaken too quickly, as too much of the starch is used by the amylase metabolizing. Development times should be shortened. Ideally the falling number should be between 240 and 280. Above 300, it becomes difficult to make good quality breads, and the same applies to a falling number below 220.

Gluten extensibility, elasticity, quality, amount
The amount of protein in flour provides an indication of its nature and ability or limitation of gluten formation and subsequent strength. Pastry flours have a low percentage of protein (e.g. around 8 to 10%), while bread flours have a higher percentage (ranging from 10 to 14%). However, just as important as the quantity of proteins available is the nature or quality of the proteins and this is expressed in terms of a W-value in professional baking. It is an indication of strength, as described above, but also of extensibility and elasticity. To make a baguette, for instance, a dough piece is stretched to considerable length, without tearing it and thus damaging its internal structure – the gluten formed

in the dough should be easily extensible. Dough which is too extensible, however, will also lose its strength more easily. To retain its shape, dough requires some elasticity as well, a propensity to "spring" back to its previous state. A dough that is too elastic will not allow shaping at all or will require long resting times between *pré-façonnage* and *façonnage*. It will be difficult to make an extended shape such as a baguette. Baking is likely to be irregular as well, rather than having it develop evenly in the oven. The dough can become too springy and it might burst open only in part, or not on the *grigne*, as the gluten is not yet sufficiently extensible to contain the rapid increase in volume of gas inside the dough while baking.

Thus, it is important to understand that all flour has specific levels of elasticity and extensibility, and therefore behaves differently. You might want to choose a flour that suits your needs. Indicators such as "flour for focaccia" or "flour for pizza" may serve to tell you that the gluten will be relatively extensible, rather than elastic. If you do not have a choice, or you do not have information available on the flour, you can make adjustments while going along. Autolyse serves to increase the extensibility of a dough, as does an increase in hydration level; shortening or skipping autolyse, or decreasing the hydration level, will make the dough springier, if needed. Proofing can be shortened when a dough is very extensible, thus avoiding the loss of strength. It can be lengthened when a dough is very strong and elastic, thus giving it time to "weaken" slightly, become more extensible and bake more regularly. And, as indicated, the time between *pré-façonnage* and *façonnage* is typically adjusted to meet the flour's need, enabling proper shaping.

Water absorption
Different flours absorb different amounts of water, leading to a similar dough consistency. Bakers sometimes prefer to work with flour that can absorb

a lot of water, simply because they can save money – the price of flour being higher than the price of water, and the bread weight being a fixed quantity.

In terms of quality, it is especially important that the level of hydration matches the flour's capacity to absorb water and that it is suitable for the kind of bread you would like to bake. For French bread, the required hydration level will be somewhere between 60 and 67%. As flour changes from harvest to harvest and its quality also depends on the time of milling and the subsequent resting before use, it is important to watch what happens to a dough and make adjustments accordingly. The speed of development should be right, as well as the consistency and strength of the dough.

If a dough is very highly hydrated, to the point that the flour is just able to absorb the water, the crumb structure will become more irregular, and in fact, when properly handled, beautiful, with large alveoli such as in *ciabatta* or the outside crust of a good pizza. In this case the crust might weaken more

quickly though, and you need to ensure that it gets adequate baking. The flavor can also be very full and well developed, as the free water molecules in the dough will be used by both yeast and enzymes, and their activity will be relatively high. It will, however, become more difficult to shape dough of this nature, and the bread will be relatively flat, as in fact is also the case with ciabatta. It may prove to be impossible to score a nice *grigne*.

For some breads, such as for the traditional *pizza bianca*, hydration should be between 85 and 95%. It is important to choose a flour that can absorb a relatively high proportion of water while retaining sufficient strength. If this is not available, slightly decrease the water percentage to obtain good results anyway.

Sometimes a flour mill will provide you with an indication of the appropriate level of hydration of a flour (expressed as a percentage relative to flour weight), based on their own testing.

Room temperature and humidity

Room temperature and humidity are two environmental factors usually outside of our control. Take the following effects into consideration.

A higher room temperature will cause the dough temperature to rise, which can make it develop too fast. When mixing, the dough temperature increases because the bowl and the flour will have a higher initial temperature. When resting, the effect will be more gradual: with time the dough will slowly move towards ambient temperature, in the end stabilizing at a few degrees warmer because of its internal activity. When shaping the dough, the effect will be quite immediate, as the smaller dough pieces quickly adjust to ambient temperature, being affected by the air temperature, the temperature of the work surface, and the temperature of your hands.

To achieve an ideal dough temperature after mixing, you can quite easily compensate for a warmer environment by using colder water. During the resting phase, you could choose a relatively cold place to put the dough, if there are such places to be found. If not, it is best to use the fridge, or to alternate putting the dough in the fridge and taking it out again if you don't want development to slow down too much. A good trick for weighing and shaping, when room temperatures are high, is to work with a relatively cold dough, by having the primary fermentation take place entirely in the fridge, or by placing the dough in the fridge during the last phase of the primary fermentation. Nonetheless, you will have to work fast, especially if batches are bigger. In a professional environment it is advisable to divide the dough into several smaller containers, working on smaller quantities at one time. Return the dough pieces to the fridge for proofing.

Likewise, if the room temperature is relatively cold, the dough will develop more slowly and it is advisable to start off with a slightly higher dough temperature, or to use a fraction more yeast. In both cases, remember that slow dough development is usually favorable to achieving good quality bread, so if you have the time, you might also simply increase the time of the primary fermentation phase.

After the bread has been baked, remember that high temperatures, over 86°F (30°C), will favor the development of mold. However, the acidity in a bread which has had sufficient development time will usually keep it fresh for a few days. Temperatures below 68°F (20°C) (e.g. in a fridge) will make the bread stale very quickly, because the starch will lose its tenderness by the process of starch retrogradation. Temperatures between 68°F (20°C) and 86°F (30°C) are ideal for the conservation of bread.

Humidity can be low or high, depending on the climate. Generally speaking, relatively elevated humidity is good while working on the dough, as it prevents a crust from forming on the dough pieces. After baking, however, it will cause the bread to become stale more quickly. The crust will become chewy and lose its *croustilliance*. The process through which the humidity from the crumb passes through the crust to the outside air will be impeded, and even the crumb quality might be compromised. These are also the reasons why bread should not be stored in a plastic bag, especially when it is still warm, but rather a paper bag which allows the bread to "breathe". Keeping the bread in plastic might also lead to mold, as the humid crust provides a more favorable environment for its development.

Low humidity makes the dough dry out very quickly while you are working on it and you will need to make sure to constantly cover it well, by using an airtight container or covering the dough pieces with a damp cloth or a polyethylene bag while they are resting. After baking, the bread will remain fresh for longer, that is, if you managed to keep the dough pieces sufficiently humid – dry pieces in the dough will dry out again very quickly after baking. The crust will remain strong and crusty, and the humidity of the crumb will be easily transferred to and absorbed by the air. If the bread was made quickly, the crumb will actually dry out, but if it has been left to rise for long enough and the dough was sufficiently hydrated, it will stay fresh and very nice to eat, also because the crust will protect the bread from drying out too much on the inside. Again, the bread can best be kept in a paper bag; it will prevent the bread from drying out excessively, while allowing it to breathe.

Too much humidity causes dough to be stickier and thus difficult to handle, especially if condensation takes place. This usually happens when a cool dough is moved to a higher temperature. The air close to the dough will be relatively cold and will not be able to contain the same amount of moisture as the warmer air around. When using a proofing cabinet in a bakery, with controlled humidity, take care to choose a humidity setting which is not too high when warming up the cabinet with cold, already shaped, dough pieces inside. Likewise, when cooling down dough in a proofing cabinet, keep the humidity level as high as possible.

A very high level of humidity can also cause the dough to develop a little faster, and the dough can become slightly more extensible or weaker, as the hydration level in the dough remains higher.

Generally speaking, if well controlled, differences in room temperature and humidity do not need to have a great impact on a dough. After baking, their impact is harder to control. Under unfavorable circumstances, it might be better to freeze bread if you want to keep it fresh for longer and put it in the oven again after taking it out of the freezer. If you just want the crust to become crusty again, you could also put bread which is one or several days old in the oven again for just a few minutes, thus letting the moisture from the crust evaporate.

Water temperature and dough temperature

The speed at which a dough develops and increases in volume, but also the chemical and physical processes taking place inside the dough, depend on the temperature of the dough. Since flour will have the ambient temperature of the place where you keep it stored, and salt and yeast are normally used in such small quantities that they do not influence the overall temperature, controlling the water temperature offers the most likely and easiest way to control the temperature of a dough. Thus, in bakeries as well as when baking at home, it is useful to measure, and possibly adjust the temperature of the water that you use. In a bakery, but even to some extent when working at home, it is also necessary to consider the heat which is transferred onto a dough while kneading or working it. The more intensive and the longer the kneading (but also the bigger the bowl, or the more the dough is handled) the more its temperature will increase. So, if you want to get a dough to a temperature of 75°F (24°C), you might want to go for quite cold water to start with, and if you would like to have a dough which is really cold, e.g. around 50°F (10°C) or 59°F (15°C), you might even have to use ice water or water from the fridge.

Dough temperature also affects the speed at which gluten strands form during mixing, and a colder dough will need more time to develop gluten. This could be precisely what you want, depending on the results you want to achieve, e.g. if you are relying on a long autolyse, long development times and folding to acquire further strength. If you want to make bread quickly, it could be a problem, as cold dough could require longer kneading.

To find out exactly which temperature you need, the only way (apart from making fairly complex calculations which assume you are perfectly aware of all variables) is to just try out one thing and measure the result, so you will have an intuitive, if not exact, idea for the next time. Also remember that although dough temperature is important, it is also possible to make adjustments in the processes following the initial mixing, for instance by placing the dough in the fridge or even in the freezer for a short time, if it turned out too warm.

Using a couche

A *couche* is a piece of linen on which the dough is left to rest (*coucher* means "to sleep") after it has been shaped. French bakeries use large pieces of linen especially fabricated for this purpose. The linen is usually rolled up, placed on a big baking tray, and then unrolled bit by bit to place the dough pieces on it, making a fold between each bread to provide some support and to prevent each loaf from touching the next. This helps breads keep their shape during proofing since, rather than flattening, they expand upwards. Also, the *couche* prevents them from sticking to the tray, so that later they can be easily lifted off for baking. When using a slow proofing phase, the *couche* may be sprinkled with some flour to prevent the bread from sticking (best is to use a rougher grind, such as the Italian *semolina di grano duro*. You only need very, very little, as it doesn't immediately absorb liquid and remains dry for a longer period of time).

At home, you might not have access to *couches* or big baking trays, nor is your fridge likely to be big enough. The trick is to make your own *couches*, by placing a regular sized cotton dishtowel on a smaller baking tray that fits inside your fridge. If the towel is too small for the tray and the amount of bread you are making, simply use a second one.

Make sure that the towel doesn't smell of soap – preferably wash it without using any soap, and keep it solely for this purpose.

You can use a *couche* even when only making a single loaf of bread. To prevent the bread from flattening, support the dishtowel at the sides using another rolled up dishtowel, for example, or the edge of the baking tray. When baking individual breads, a wicker proofing basket is an alternative to a *couche*. They operate much the same way and yield a similar result.

Put the baking tray with the breads into a large plastic bag before placing them in the fridge for long overnight proofing, so that the bread will not dry out. Make sure the plastic doesn't touch the bread. If you think it might, cover the bread with another dishtowel before putting everything in the plastic bag.

Finally, make sure you don't lay the breads too close to one another on the *couche*. They should mainly expand upwards, but there also should be room for them to expand very slightly sideways as well.

Making and using a dough peel

To get the bread onto a baking stone in your oven, you will have to move it from the *couche*, bowl, or wicker proofing basket. A fully developed bread is hard to pick up by hand. It's also not a good idea to directly place your hands in the hot oven. The trick is to first place the bread on a dough peel, as for instance used in pizzerias. A dough peel can be purchased, but also easily made at home. Buy a piece of triplex and cut it to match the size of your baking stone, sanding it at one end to make it smooth and tapered while leaving a handle on the other end.

1. There is a simple technique to get the bread from a *couche* onto your peel. Use another flat piece of wood with a stocking around it so that the dough will not stick, hold it next to the bread and pull the *couche* so that the bread rolls over onto the stocking-covered piece of wood.

2. Now transfer the bread from the piece of wood to the dough peel by rolling it from the one to the other, so that the bread is right side up again on the peel. To prevent the bread from sticking to the peel, sprinkle it with some semolina flour, or lay a piece of baking paper on top of the peel (especially useful when placing several breads in the oven at once; you can use the paper to slide them into the oven).

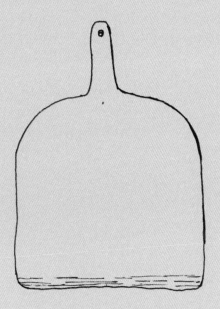

Homemade peel

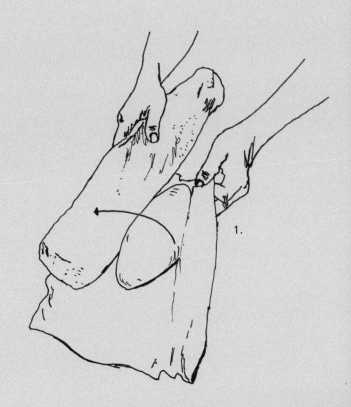

1.

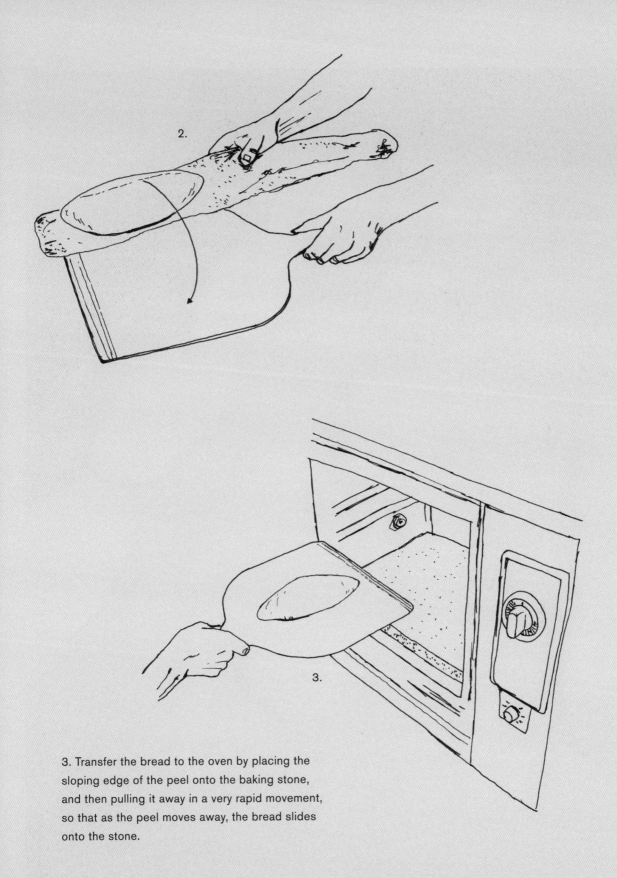

3. Transfer the bread to the oven by placing the
sloping edge of the peel onto the baking stone,
and then pulling it away in a very rapid movement,
so that as the peel moves away, the bread slides
onto the stone.

Scoring batards

Scoring bread: la grigne

La grigne, the grimace, is the score the baker makes just before the bread goes into the oven and which opens up beautifully while baking. In France, it is considered the baker's signature. When the bread goes into the oven and is baked on the stone floor, an immense amount of heat is transferred almost instantaneously to the dough. The crust will start to form almost immediately, slowed only by the steam, which is usually added at the beginning of baking, and enables it to stay flexible a bit longer. The bread will start to rise in volume only after a few minutes, the crust still being a little stretchable, then will burst open precisely at its weakest spot: where the baker has made the score.

The score thus allows the bread to expand further, increasing in volume evenly and developing an open structure. Also, you will find that while the rest of the bread develops a strong, thick crust, this part of the crust will be very light and perfectly crunchy.

To score bread, use a razor blade (*lame*), fixed to the flat end of a tablespoon, for instance. Use only the tip of the blade and hold it at a slight angle. Make quick moves, so that the bread scores cleanly, without sticking to the blade. Do not score too deeply. A very light touch will do, as otherwise the bread will flatten where it has been scored, losing its strength.

The bread will expand when baking, so a very slightly diagonal cut on the top of the bread will eventually go all the way from one side to the other when the bread expands in the oven. For a baguette you could, for instance, make three incisions, at a slight angle, partly overlapping each time.

To achieve a good *grigne*, the bread must have enough force when put into the oven. Proper *façonnage* is essential to provide enough surface tension on the dough. Also, an overdeveloped bread dough will flatten, rather than expand, in the oven. And an underdeveloped dough will not yet contain sufficient gases to "explode", and the *grigne* will only open partway.

The humidity in the oven must be just right. Too much humidity, and the crust will remain soft and extensible all over – the bread will rise, but the *grigne* will not open up. Too little humidity, and even the part where the bread has been scored might not develop a strong crust before the bread starts to increase in volume. The bread will stay small and have a few irregular openings.

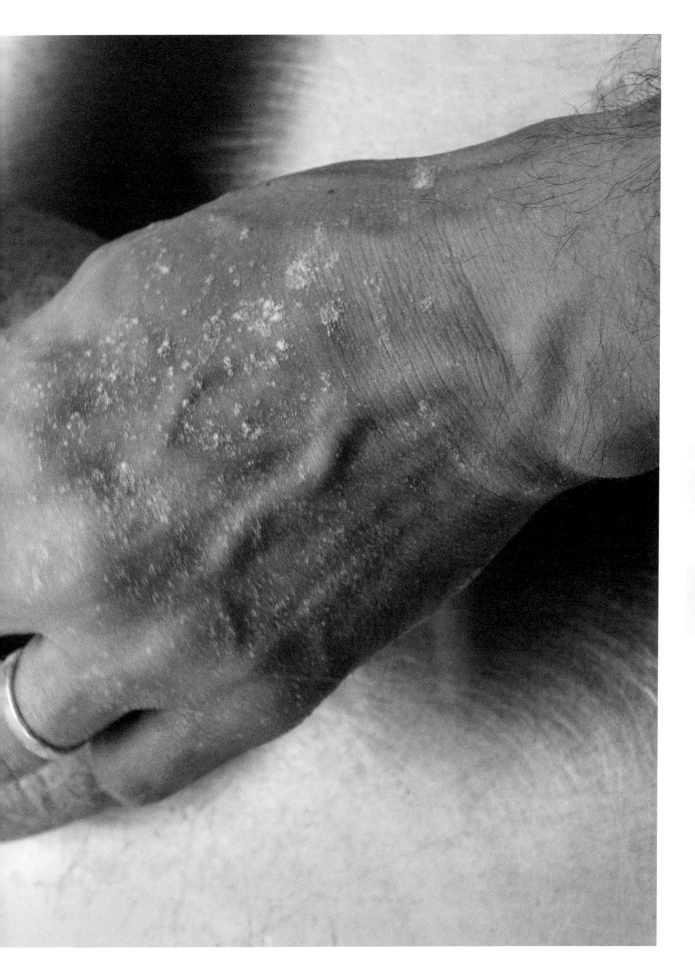

Acknowledgements

I wrote this book with a lot of joy. After years of baking, it became a part of me to such an extent that I was able to write in cafés and from terraces in sunny Alghero or sometimes less sunny Paris. Places where I could withdraw from the daily work in our bakery, alone, without an oven, without reference books.

Nevertheless my gratitude immediately goes to the authors who have inspired me, and most particularly: Peter Reinhart, author of the inspiring book *The Bread Baker's Apprentice*, Daniel Wing and Alan Scott for their book *The Bread Builders*, written with the passion of home bakers in search of the best bread imaginable, and Raymond Calvel for his classic work *Le Goût Du Pain (The Taste of Bread)*, the title of the book indicating what it should all revolve around.

I would also like to thank the bakers in our bakery who gave me the time to write this book, and especially to Anna Sokha, the heart of our bakery; Charlie de Saint Jores, for his passion and for one of the recipes in this book; Thomas de Jong, who just like Anna appears in some of the pictures; and Mark Verweij and Paulien Koning for proofreading and test baking the recipes. Thank you also to Erwin Hurenkamp, who as bakery manager during the period of making this book provided the love that a family company cannot do without. In that respect, my gratitude goes to our entire team, past and present, and especially to Merel Coolen for her contribution: the video promoting this book.

I am also greatly indebted to the bakeries where I have worked, or the ones I was able to join for a day or a night on my travels. I started as an apprentice at Hartog in Amsterdam and then it was Menno 't Hoen who gave me the confidence to work as a baker in a small team at his former artisanal French bakery in Rotterdam. I worked for a longer period with Gosselin in Paris, and ever so briefly worked at Panificio Piras in Sardegna, and at Gentillini Pasticerria and Forno Campo de' Fiori in Rome during my travels. And for my first introduction to wood-fired baking I would like to thank Chico and Manuela Ramos in Moncarapacho, Portugal, for generously sharing their knowledge with me.

A team of individuals has worked towards the production of the original edition of this book, making choices that were not always safe or obvious, and which have allowed this book to become its authentic self. For this I am grateful to Paul Brandt, the exceptionally committed publisher who gave me the freedom and confidence to develop the book, and to his whole team for the support. To Rachelle Klaassen, involved from the very beginning with the graphic design and development of the book, and for whom graphic design not only entails giving existing work its form, but also creating the work itself. To Inga Powilleit for her photos that do much more than simply depict and are so evocative on their own terms. My agent for the Dutch edition Christiaan Boesenach from Sebes and Bisseling immediately understood the value of this book and has stayed involved with every step along the way to its publication. Hélène Lesger, Ellen Sanders and Yvette van Boven were all crucially involved in the early stages of the book. And to Justin Gosker for his insightful and astute awareness of all of the visual and material aspects of this book.

I first wrote this book in English, then translated it into Dutch for the Dutch edition. For publishing this English edition, I'm indebted once again to Hélène Lesger of HL Books. Her love of books, her enthusiasm right from the very start when I first gave her my manuscript, as well as her appreciation of the baked goods from our bakery, combined to make this edition possible. I also would like to thank Kay Dixon for editing the manuscript, and Wouter Eertink for incorporating the English text into the original design made by Rachelle Klaassen.

Finally, but actually first, I would like to thank my brother Marco, who recognized the potential of my baking experiments before I regarded them in such a way, and with whom I started our bakery. My parents, Leidie and Rudo, supported us in our endeavors in the same way as they supported and encouraged us in every aspect of our lives. My beloved Alex, not just for the love that is necessary to write a book and subsequently publish it and share it with the world, but also for her critical gaze that I can trust when making difficult choices. And our son Ezra, still too young to let me free up time to work on this book, but old enough to share my joy in books.

Index